D1561152

THE MUSIC OF JAMES SCOTT

James Scott, ca. 1903. From the cover of "A Summer Breeze."

THE MUSIC OF JAMES SCOTT

Edited by Scott DeVeaux and
William Howland Kenney

SMITHSONIAN INSTITUTION PRESS ━ WASHINGTON AND LONDON

Editor: Aaron Appelstein
Supervisory Editor: Duke Johns
Designer: Linda McKnight
Music Examples and Autography: John I. Davis, Music-Book Associates

Library of Congress Cataloging-in-Publication Data
Scott, James, 1885–1938.
    [Works. 1992]
    The music of James Scott / edited by Scott DeVeaux and William Howland Kenney.
    p. of music.
    Includes bibliographical references and index.
    ISBN 1–56098–143–1 (alk. paper)
    1. Ragtime music. I. DeVeaux, Scott Knowles. II. Kenney, William Howland. III. Title.
  M3.S4 1992   91-37955

British Library Cataloguing-in-Publication Data is available

Manufactured in the United States of America
99 98 97 96 95 94 93 92 5 4 3 2 1

CONTENTS

ACKNOWLEDGMENTS

THE EDITORS WOULD LIKE TO THANK the following ragtime artists and sheet music collectors for their assistance in locating copies of the scores: George Foley, John Hasse, David Jasen, Michael Montgomery, Trebor Tichenor, Galen Wilkes, Tex Wyndham, and Richard Zimmerman. They also wish to express their appreciation to Richard Crawford, John Hasse, and the late Martin Williams for their advice, encouragement, and inspiration for this project.

JAMES SCOTT: AN INTRODUCTION

William Howland Kenney

JAMES SCOTT, ONE OF "THE TWO GREATEST ragtime composers," fashioned rhythmically ebullient, technically challenging scores that enrich the core literature of classic ragtime. Although some of Scott's compositions—"Grace and Beauty," "Ragtime Oriole," "Sunburst Rag," and "Climax Rag"—occupy a prominent position in the literature, relatively little has been written about the composer or about the relationship of his works to the historical and cultural forces of his time. Recent cultural analysis of ragtime performance has emphasized its connections to the demi-monde of turn-of-the-century urban saloon life. But even though James Scott worked in such performance environments, his life and published scores reflect a complex African American mixture of small-town, late nineteenth-century midwestern culture and early twentieth-century popular music.[1]

---

1. The estimate of Scott's relative importance as a ragtime composer appears in John Hasse, "Ragtime from the Top," in *Ragtime: Its History, Composers, and Music*, ed. John Edward Hasse (New York: Schirmer Books, 1985), 20, and Rudi Blesh and Harriet Janis, *They All Played Ragtime*, 4th ed. (New York: Oak Publications, 1971), 112–16. Edward A. Berlin, *Reflections and Research on Ragtime*, I.S.A.M. Monographs, no. 24 (Brooklyn, N.Y.: Institute for Studies in American Music, 1987), analyzes the connections of ragtime to New York saloons, music halls, and cabarets.

James Sylvester Scott was born in Neosho (Newton County), Missouri, on 12 February 1885. He was the second of six children and the first son of James Scott and Molly Thomas Scott, who had migrated to southwestern Missouri from North Carolina after their marriage in 1878. Scott's father, a manual laborer, and grandfather were from North Carolina; his mother was born in Texas in 1863.[2] Scott's parents arrived in Missouri at the time of the "Kansas exodus" of ex-slaves from the South between 1879 and 1881. Most of the freedmen had been victims of economic and legal exploitation after Reconstruction troops were withdrawn in the Compromise of 1877. Suffering through an economic depression that hit the poorest hardest, many moved to St. Louis, Missouri, and then to several historic black settlements like Nicodemus and Wyandott, Kansas. The Scotts, however, chose to settle in Neosho in the extreme southwestern corner of Missouri, part of the tri-state lead and zinc mining district of Missouri, southeastern Kansas, and northeastern Oklahoma. The family moved about 150 miles away to Ottawa, Kansas, in 1899 but resettled in Neosho in 1901.[3]

James Scott spent his youth and the better part of his adult years in southwestern Missouri, an area nestled in rolling hills between the Oklahoma border and the Ozark mountains. It was a place of great beauty, an idyllic environment with a mild, dry climate, deep rushing rivers, orchards, strawberry fields, and vast forests. It was also home to the prosperous middle-class communities of Neosho, Joplin, and Carthage. Scott lived with his family in Neosho until 1902 when at age seventeen he struck off on his own for Carthage. He resided in Carthage during his most productive years, coming to terms with the town's powerful drive for a middle-class respectability framed in proudly stolid new government buildings, schools, railroad stations, and churches, as well as an opera house built with the massive stone blocks cut from local quarries. The Carthage *Evening Press* touted the settled civility of paved streets, water and sewage systems, and the telephone; early twentieth-century south-

2. Galen Wilkes, "James Scott's Birthdate Discovered!" *Rag Times* 19 (1985): 1. Marvin Van Gilder, "James Scott," in *Ragtime*, ed. Hasse, 137–45, provides valuable data on Scott. See also Blesh and Janis, *They All Played Ragtime*, 112–15.

3. Nell Irvin Painter, *Exodusters: Black Migration to Kansas after Reconstruction* (New York: Knopf, 1977), chaps. 12 and 15; Robert G. Athearn, *In Search of Canaan: Black Migration to Kansas, 1879–80* (Lawrence: Regents Press of Kansas, 1978); Joseph H. Taylor, "The Movement of Negroes from North Carolina, 1876–1894," *North Carolina Historical Review* 33 (1956): 45–65. Information on Scott's movements in Van Gilder, "James Scott," should be compared with that in the Carthage *Evening Press* (hereafter *CEP*), 6 May 1903, 3. Milton D. Rafferty, *Historical Atlas of Missouri* (Norman: University of Oklahoma Press, 1982), and idem, *Missouri: A Geography* (Boulder, Colo.: Westview Press, 1983), describe the tri-state mining district.

western Missouri wanted refined, respectable music to accompany its middle-class order. With typical booster pride Carthage thought of itself as "the seat of culture, education, and refinement for Jasper County and the southwest" and found satisfaction in its brand-new Carnegie Library, summer Chautauqua, Calhoun Music College, Carthage Chorus, Jasper County Chorus, Light Guard Band, many churches, and relative lack of saloons. (There were only three saloons in 1903, compared with "wicked Joplin's" fifty-five, one of which was run by a woman known as "Big Jim" Quinlan).[4]

Scott was introduced to music at home in Neosho where his mother passed on her approach to music to her children, teaching all six of them to play the piano by ear. James, Jr., was the only one who subsequently took lessons and became musically literate. He profited fully from a sketchy musical education, taking, according to Marvin Van Gilder, "some thirty formal lessons in classical piano with application to the developing idiom to be known as ragtime" from John Coleman, a saloon pianist and music teacher. According to Missouri newspapers, however, an unnamed Joplin physician, for whom Scott tended horses, gave him "twelve lessons on the piano and this comprises his sole musical education."[5] He also may have studied music at the segregated Lincoln School in Neosho, but, like most blacks of his era, he seems to have taught himself most of what he needed to know.

Even finding a piano on which to practice was a problem, because the Scotts were too poor to own one. Like the young Joplin, who practiced on pianos in the homes of white people for whom his mother was a maid, the young Scott sought out keyboards in neighbors' homes, public buildings, and local music stores. When he was fifteen, his parents brought back to their new home in Neosho a small reed pump organ that had belonged to an aunt and uncle. The brand name is not known, but inexpensive Estey organs (harmoniums) were popular among poor but upwardly mobile blacks. Booker T. Washington, the acknowledged spokesperson for turn-of-the-century American blacks, feared that such musical instruments were an extravagance for the poor; many families paid fifty cents down and fifty cents per week for the rest of their lives to own an Estey pump organ.

4. Walter Williams, *The State of Missouri, an Autobiography* (Carthage, Mo.: E. W. Stevens, 1904), 309–10, 412–13, 460–61, describes Carthage and Jasper County. *CEP*, 4 June 1904, 2, contains the quoted cultural depiction. See also *CEP*, 8 May 1903, 3; 24 June 1903, 5; 15 Sept. 1903, 6; 17 June 1907, 4; 25 Nov. 1907, 4; 6 Jan. 1908, 4 (identifying "Big Jim" Quinlan); 17 Jan. 1908, 8; and 27 Aug. 1909, 6.

5. *CEP*, 11 Feb. 1903, 4; and St. Louis [Mo.], *Post-Dispatch*, 8 Mar. 1903, sec. 4, 6, refer to the unnamed horse-owning teacher. John Coleman is mentioned in Van Gilder, "James Scott," 138.

Despite Washington's concern, Eubie Blake, W. C. Handy, and James Scott—all of whom learned on family harmoniums—went on to build substantial careers in music. Eventually Scott's father bought a used upright piano, and his son got to know it well.[6]

Despite southwestern Missouri's distance from such major centers of black culture as Kansas City and St. Louis, Scott would have had little trouble discovering the geographically mobile world of midwestern black pianists, whose music combined classical, march, and folk styles in novel ways. An intense period of railroad and electric trolley construction allowed greater, freer movement to the entire population. Faster, cheaper transportation brought within reach major centers of leisure-time activities and nightlife like Joplin, Sedalia, Kansas City, Jefferson City, and Columbia (where the Allen Music Company published Scott's "Great Scott Rag" in 1909). Scott would have had access to a network of ragtime pianists; this network included contacts in such main centers as Kansas City even before the publication of his "Kansas City Rag" in 1907. Scott Joplin, Otis Saunders, Tom Turpin, Arthur Marshall, Scott Hayden, Louis Chauvin, John W. "Blind" Boone, and many other roving ragtime pianists played throughout the state. Boone, a former child prodigy whose "Rag Medleys" provide the clearest published evidence of the links between ragtime and the folk tradition, visited southwestern Missouri on more than one occasion. His appearance in Joplin's First Christian Church for a year-end concert in 1903, for example, drew a capacity crowd that heard him perform classics of European concert music as well as "Plantation melodies." In an era of strict racial segregation, these African American musicians and entertainers formed a mobile, racially based school of piano music that drew on several different musical traditions.[7]

A young African American musician like Scott had several career possibilities. He could pursue, as he did, a "respectable" career in teaching music, playing in orchestras, and directing church choirs within the black community. In addition, although there is scant evidence of it, he could

---

6. Washington wrote: "In these cabin homes [of the poor] I often found [extravagant and irrational purchases]. . . . I remember that on one occasion when I went into one of these cabins for dinner, when I sat down to the table for a meal with the four members of the family, I noticed that, while there were five of us at the table, there was but one fork for the five of us to use. Naturally there was an awkward pause on my part. In the opposite corner of that same cabin was an organ for which the people told me they were paying sixty dollars in monthly instalments. One fork, and a sixty-dollar organ! . . . The organ, of course, was rarely used for want of a person who could play upon it." Booker T. Washington, *Up from Slavery: An Autobiography* (Garden City, N.Y.: Doubleday, 1915), 113–14.

7. John W. Boone Papers, Western Historical Manuscripts Collection, Missouri State Historical Society, Columbia, Mo.

have worked in the demimonde of saloon pianists, who entertained whites and blacks with the latest popular styles. The new ragtime offered Scott an attractive way of combining aspects of these two contrasting worlds by developing the compositional possibilities of a distinctly African American music that reached into the American mainstream through points of contact with marches, popular song, and dance music. Scott's handwritten scores and the published compositions that followed also provided him with the social status denied to saloon pianists and served as a buffer against the unsavory sides of nightlife entertainment.

Scott's career as a ragtime composer got under way in 1903 when Charles R. Dumars, city alderman, director of the Carthage Light Guard Band from 1885, and owner of Dumars Music at 109 South Main Street, arranged for Scott to break into the music business. In that year Dumars underwrote the printing of Scott's "Summer Breeze"—originally titled "A Summer Zephyr"—and thus established the young pianist as a published composer whose influence reached beyond the saloons. The town newspaper reported that "the arrangement is original and catchy. His counter points [*sic*] are especially fine and while the music is popular yet it is of a good grade. Jim's manuscript is as clear as type and he arranged it without any assistance from others." According to a St. Louis newspaper report, a Philadelphia firm had placed an advance order for 1,000 copies. Dumars, moreover, paid Scott a royalty on each copy sold.[8]

The Carthage *Evening Press* appeared to have little difficulty understanding the idea of intrinsic musical talent, labeling Scott a "musical prodigy," but it did express some surprise that an African American could read music and even compose "good grade" popular scores. That Scott should play the piano well was less surprising than his impressive mastery of musical notation:

> His piano playing is remarkable in spite of his limited training, and his technique is said to be exceptionally fine. His use of the left hand is his strong point, and he takes to piano playing naturally.
>
> Jim reads music very readily at sight. In composing, he plays his piece over and over, strengthening the weak places and toning down those too strong. Then he plays it through and sits down and writes it out complete without going back to the piano.[9]

---

8. *CEP*, 11 Feb. 1903, 4, describes "A Summer Breeze." Royalty arrangements are documented in St. Louis *Post-Dispatch*, 8 Mar. 1903, sec. 4, 6.

9. *CEP*, 11 Feb. 1903, 4.

In 1904 Scott, who had been working as a porter and "[shoe]shine artist" in Hoyt Gierhart's barbershop, gained a further foothold in the music profession when Dumars hired him to sweep floors, wash windows, frame pictures, and demonstrate pianos at his music store. This long-lasting, paid position extended through Dumars's partnership with Carthage mayor C. B. Gammon and anchored Scott's career as a ragtime composer.

Dumars kept Baldwin, Strick & Zeidler, Haddorf, Ellington, Hamilton, Clarendon, Howard, Temple, and Monarch pianos in a special storage room, giving Scott an ideal place to practice, compose, and perform for the public. When Dumars advertised pianos around the region, he sent Scott along to perform on them. He also provided Scott with a model of musical entrepreneurship and a wealth of musical contacts. In addition to "A Summer Breeze" (1903), Dumars subsequently published Scott's "Fascinator—March and Two-Step" (1903) and "On the Pike—(A Rag-time Two-Step)" (1904). A few years later he contributed sentimental lyrics to two of Scott's popular songs as well: "She's My Girl from Anaconda" (1909) and "Sweetheart Time" (1909). The former was planned as a feature for the popular Carthage singer Joseph Stebbins as part of a charity minstrel show by the Elks Club. Music dealers in Kansas City, St. Louis, Chicago, New York, and Boston placed orders for the sheet music. [10]

In the summer of 1904 Scott had an opportunity to appear with "Blind" Boone, who had come to town to help promote the Missouri State Negro Improvement Association (MSNIA), a cultural uplift organization that had scheduled a meeting in Carthage's Chautauqua Park. The content of their impromptu concert at Dumars's store reveals how freely ragtime, march, and classical musics intermingled at the time. As reported in the local press:

> A handful of people which grew to a throng as the entertainment continued occupied the Dumars music store Saturday morning when Blind Boone, Jimmie Scott, and Sousa's band were the attractions. Boone chanced to call at the Dumars store to see his professional friend Jimmie Scott, the young colored man who enjoys a reputation as both composer and piano player. Mr. Scott played for Mr. Boone and in the course of his program did a new and certainly original stunt.
>
> A gramophone containing a Sousa band piece was turned on and Jimmie played a clever piano accompaniment which really made good music. Boone was delighted and before the selection ended said that he

10. *CEP*, 10 Apr. 1909, 3.

had to get his own hand in. He went to the piano and placing his hand on the treble made his nimble fingers fly over the keys in such a manner as to produce an accompaniment to the whole business which sounded like a piccolo. It seemed as if a whole orchestra was there and the audience was bewildered.

Both Boone and Scott followed with a number of selections both rag time and classical. Boone proved himself a rag time player equal to his unquestioned ability in the higher class of music.[11]

Scott, Boone, the audience, and the newspaper reporter compared ragtime with, and distinguished it from, this other style (i.e., "classical"). In its regular gossip column, written in country dialect, the town newspaper labeled Scott "Our Local Mozart."[12]

Scott soon began a long-term engagement as keyboard performer at Lakeside Amusement Park in Webb City, halfway between Carthage and Joplin on one of the several electric railroad lines in the area. Although parks and recreational facilities were racially segregated in Missouri, African Americans were admitted on special days and as entertainers for white patrons. Scott played piano for the silent films shown in Lakeside's theater; he also rented the Lakeside Dance Pavilion, where he organized dances and performed for fellow blacks. Years later, in 1914, Scott wrote "Take Me Out to Lakeside," to which Ida B. Miller, whose husband owned tourist cabins in the area, contributed romantic lyrics. Published by Ball Music Company of Carthage, this old-fashioned, waltz-time promotional song, like the earlier pieces published by Dumars and Dumars-Gammon, reflected Scott's participation in local musical enterprise.[13]

Scott also gained exposure to regional musicians through the Carthage Light Guard Band, which Charles Dumars directed from 1885 to 1920 with only one interruption. Brass bands and concert wind ensembles like this one were community institutions in towns and villages across the country. Dumars sought out the best musicians in other towns and arranged jobs for them in Carthage, modestly swelling the population of a town committed to competition with Joplin. Over the years the town sent its band on trips to Denver, Boston, Pittsburgh, and Louisville. In each city it advertised the advantages of living in Carthage, Missouri.[14]

---

11. *CEP,* 15 Aug. 1904, 4.

12. *CEP,* 8 May 1915, 2.

13. *CEP,* 16 Aug. 1915, 8.

14. *CEP,* 18 June 1907, 4; Charles Hamm, *Music in the New World* (New York: W. W. Norton, 1983), 288–306; H. Wiley Hitchcock, *Music in the United States: A Historical Introduction,* 3d ed. (Englewood Cliffs, N.J.: Prentice-Hall, 1988), 122–30.

Figure 1. Dance Pavilion, Lakeside Amusement Park, Webb City, Missouri, ca. 1910. Photo courtesy of Marvin L. Van Gilder.

Figure 2. Interior of Dance Pavilion, Lakeside Amusement Park, ca. 1910. Photo courtesy of Marvin L. Van Gilder.

Scott lived in an era when American concert/military bands still functioned as both concert groups and dance orchestras. As a concert group the Light Guard Band played marches, waltzes, and light classics for the yearly Carthage Chautauqua in Chautauqua Park and presented, through the subscription of town merchants, weekly concerts throughout the summer on the town square. On 11 July 1904 the Light Guard Band performed an orchestral arrangement of Scott's "On the Pike." According to a local review, "It sounds well as band music and the rendition Saturday night was well worth the applause which the hearers gave."[15] Socially active black Missourians would have questioned the rag's association with "the Pike," the commercial concession area of the 1903 Louisiana Purchase Exposition in St. Louis. The exposition discriminated against blacks by refusing to provide them with restaurants or accommodations. The St. Louis *Palladium,* a black newspaper, urged that "Afro-Americans with any pride" refuse to attend.[16]

When performing as a dance band for the militia and for citizens at Lakeside Dance Pavilion or at black dances in the town armory, the Dumars orchestra combined established nineteenth-century social dance music with the more rhythmically heated dance steps of the early twentieth century. Throughout the nineteenth century, Americans had danced "pattern" or "figure" steps like the cotillion, requiring memorization of complex and stylized group movements. Gradually, however, the country turned to less complicated couple dances like the polka and the waltz, which also permitted more bodily contact between dancing partners.

At the turn of the century, wind ensembles featured the two-step, a fast ballroom dance introduced in the late 1880s. In the two-step the man would either face his partner or stand slightly behind and to the left of her (the woman's hands raised above her head to take his). Initially the step was performed to standard marches like Sousa's "Washington Post" (1889), which has a skipping $\frac{6}{8}$ rhythm simulating a light, springing march step. (The dance subsequently became associated with $\frac{2}{4}$ and $\frac{4}{4}$ time.) Sousa's march and the dance step inspired many imitations, such as Arthur Pryor's "Ye Boston Tea Party Two Step" (1896). Scott's "Fascinator—March and Two-Step" and "On the Pike" were arranged for wind ensemble and were performed at dances as well as in concert.[17]

As an African American musician Scott would not have been allowed

15. *CEP,* 11 July 1904, 2.
16. St. Louis *Palladium,* 8 Oct. 1904, 1. A representative band program under Dumars's direction included the following pieces (*CEP,* 18 June 1904, 5):

March—"Buckeye State" . . . . Yingling
Medley—"Superba" . . . . Dalbey
Waltz—"Trinity College" . . . . Missud
Military Sketch—"The Reveille" . . . . Laurendeau
Selection—"Prince of Pilsen" . . . . Luders
March—"Uncle Sammy" . . . . Holtzman

17. *CEP,* 5 Apr. 1904, 3; 11 July 1904, 2; *New Grove Dictionary of American Music,* s.v. "Two-step."

to conduct Dumars's all-white Light Guard Band, even when they performed one of his own compositions. Early twentieth-century communities like Carthage insisted upon independent, duplicate sets of institutions: a separate "colored" baseball team, the Carthage Eagles; segregated saloons, pool halls, restaurants, and movie theaters; separate occasions reserved for blacks in vaudeville theaters and out at Lakeside; and, inevitably, separate wind ensembles. One of Scott's pet projects, therefore, was the organization of an all-black marching and concert band to provide black musicians a chance to perform and black audiences with musical entertainment. With relatively few local musicians at hand, he recruited additional players from Greenfield, Joplin, and Webb City. The sixteen members of this band played concerts under Scott's direction in Carthage's Carter Park, at the county fair, for Joplin's African Methodist Episcopal (A.M.E.) Church, for dances and roller skating in the Armory, and in honor of black draftees departing for World War I. Scott hoped to make it "the best colored musical organization in this part of the country." To supply dance music at less expense, he also created from within the band a four-piece dance combo composed of piano, violin, cornet, and trap drums.[18]

The composition of scores and arrangements for social dance music had long offered an area of interracial cooperation between black musician-composers and white social dance instructors. Black musicians such as J. R. Conner, James Hemmenway, Isaac Hazzard, and Edward De Roland in Philadelphia; William Brady and Walter F. Craig in New York; Henry F. Williams in Boston; and Joseph W. Postlewaite in St. Louis organized orchestras and, allying themselves with white social dancing teachers, composed dance music for publication.

Five of Scott's collaborations with Dumars were finally published in arrangements for solo piano. These works represent an extension into the early twentieth century of the nineteenth-century tradition of interracial musical scores. Dumars, and later St. Louis publisher John Stark, continued the role of earlier white dancing instructors in encouraging African American composers in this direction. Given the divisive role of racial segregation in early twentieth-century musical performance, these published piano scores created a small but important area of interracial cooperation.[19]

---

18. *CEP*, 16 Feb. 1903, 6; 15 Aug. 1906, 4; 31 Oct. 1907, 6; 29 Feb. 1916, 4.
19. Samuel A. Floyd, Jr., and Marsha J. Reisser, "Social Dance Music of Black Composers in the Nineteenth Century and the Emergence of Classic Ragtime," *Black Perspective in Music* 8 (1980): 161–93.

In the most important move of his career, Scott made contact with the influential white St. Louis publisher John Stillwell Stark, who in 1899 had published Scott Joplin's "Maple Leaf Rag." Scott and Stark could not have become close associates, since Stark lived in New York City from 1905 to 1910, by which time his company had issued eight of Scott's scores. Moreover, Scott mailed his manuscripts to the Stark Music Company and was proud that his scores were selected from "a flood of" unsolicited manuscripts.[20]

The Stark Music Company issued twenty-nine of the thirty-eight scores published during Scott's lifetime, including twenty-five rags, three waltzes, and one song. "Frog Legs Rag" (1906), their first collaboration, was a best-seller and cemented their business partnership. Stark continued to publish Scott's rags for sixteen years; "Broadway Rag" (1922) was both Scott's and Stark's last publication. Over the long run Scott built his reputation as a composer on his association with John Stark. However, he established his professional independence from the publisher by occasionally selling his scores to other firms, namely, the Allen Music Company of Columbia, Missouri ("Blind" Boone's publisher), the Will L. Livernash Company of Kansas City, and the Ball Music Company of Carthage. On one occasion he even commented to the local paper that he had not yet decided to accept Stark's offer to publish "Kansas City Rag" (1907)—although he eventually did.[21]

Scott's inspiration, Scott Joplin, also owed his prominence to Stark. But Joplin came to resent the publisher's limiting influence over the complexity and spirit of music that reached the public as "ragtime." Stark, for example, initially resisted publishing Joplin's extended folk ballet *The Ragtime Dance,* which was sure to lose money. In any event James Scott seems not to have shared Joplin's drive to extend the ragtime idiom to other genres.[22]

Scott's rags both reflected and encouraged the increasingly vigorous, rhythmically uninhibited, irreverent musical spirit that swept the nation from 1890 to 1929. But performing within the mainstream of local vernacular traditions, Scott also inherited elements of genteel musical tastes that cut across racial lines. The genteel tradition, however diluted by its passage from the East Coast into the Midwest, clearly ruled Carthage's official cultural life and helped shape ragtime into a more proper vernacu-

---

20. *CEP,* 28 June 1906, 6; 9 Aug. 1906, 4.
21. *CEP,* 9 Aug. 1906, 4.
22. James Haskins with Kathleen Benson, *Scott Joplin* (Garden City, N.Y.: Doubleday, 1978), 99–106.

lar music. Scott's ragtime scores encouraged a more intellectual approach to emotional expression by harnessing those dangerous saloon-style improvisations within a notational system and ordered structure. Historians Neil Leonard and Edward Berlin have shown that the rakish, uninhibited qualities of ragtime, strongly associated in the public mind with gaslight saloons, provoked a repressive backlash among guardians of the nation's musical propriety. In this sense ragtime publishers like Dumars, Gammon, and Stark and ragtime composers James Scott and Scott Joplin all channeled the volatile, improvisational side of the ragtime experience into the more disciplined medium of the printed page. They thus extended ragtime in sheet music form to a broad middle-class audience that would have avoided it in live performance.[23]

Political pressures from black community leaders who opposed demeaning racist stereotypes served to reinforce the genteel strain in vernacular music. Across the nation blacks suffered many injustices—lynching, denial of voting rights, labor exploitation, racially segregated ghettos, and unequal school systems. Lynching was common in Missouri. It raged uncomfortably close to James Scott when, in 1903, a Joplin mob battered through the wall of the town jailhouse and extracted Thomas Gilyard, a black accused of killing a police officer, and hanged him from a telephone pole two blocks away. Three years later a Carthage mob nearly lynched a prisoner named Estil Butler for punching jailer Ed Hansford. Three months later the Carthage militia was called to Springfield to help quell violent mobs who hanged several black men for alleged crimes that subsequently proved imaginary. Unknown terrorists opened fire on tents sheltering blacks in nearby Monett, and one refugee from Springfield reported being threatened at every stop on the railroad line to Carthage. Trying to put the best gloss possible on a terrifying state of affairs, the editor of the Carthage paper approvingly quoted Booker T. Washington's opinion that "the American Negro's future seems brighter today because his present condition is about as bad as it well could be."[24]

It is not hard to imagine why black leaders, led by Booker T. Washington, national spokesperson for American Negroes and principal of Tuskegee Institute, counseled a cautious, gradual approach to racial better-

---

23. Neil Leonard, "The Reactions to Ragtime," in *Ragtime*, ed. Hasse, 102–13; Edward A. Berlin, *Ragtime: A Musical and Cultural History* (Berkeley and Los Angeles: University of California Press, 1980), chap. 2.
24. Neosho *Times*, 23 Apr. 1903, 3; *CEP*, 16 Apr. 1903, 1, 6; 16 Jan. 1906, 1; 16 Apr. 1906, 5; 3 Dec. 1906, 4; 4 June 1910, 2 (quoting Washington).

ment—economic self-help through vocational training, along with thrift, sobriety, racial solidarity, and stable, secure trades.[25]

Washington, invited as keynote speaker to a special all-black Chautauqua in Carthage, advocated the preservation of old plantation music— the spirituals—through organized choirs made up of voices trained in "vocal culture." The nationally influential leader sent carefully trained groups like the Tuskegee Singers on fundraising tours of the North. At Tuskegee he encouraged the adaptation of black folk traditions to the structures of European concert music. The African British composer Samuel Coleridge-Taylor was his favorite, particularly "at this time, when interest in the plantation songs seems to be dying out with the generation that gave them birth, when the Negro song is in too many minds associated with 'rag' music and the more reprehensible 'coon' song."[26]

Even though Washington declared ragtime less racially offensive than "coon" songs, he never endorsed this music. Washington disapproved of the increasingly popular saloons and wine bars in which ragtime was often played and feared the adverse influence of these giddy, decadent environments on the morals of Tuskegee students. His views probably inspired sentiments at the all-black George R. Smith College in Sedalia, Missouri, whose newspaper cautioned its readers against an unthinking embrace of any music performed primarily in "wine halls" and brothels.[27]

The moral dilemma and drama involved in ragtime's association with the swinging doors divided the Scott family, separating James from his brother Douglas, reputedly a fast-living, dissipated saloon pianist. Douglas rebelled against the Washington-influenced education he received at George R. Smith College and died prematurely in 1918, at age twenty-six. James Scott spent most of his career as a performer of a rebellious new music whose sensibility reflected some of the irreverent, clearly dangerous qualities of saloons, music halls, wine bars, and brothels. But he took ingredients of working-class saloon music and transformed them into the core of a new serious composed music. Washington would have approved of the lofty ambitions of this endeavor, of Scott's refusal to compose in racial stereotypes, of his carefully crafted harmonic progressions, and of his advocacy of musical literacy. In all these respects classic ragtime (in the

25. August Meier, *Negro Thought in America, 1880–1915: Racial Ideologies in the Age of Booker T. Washington* (Ann Arbor: University of Michigan Press, 1964), 1–118.

26. *The Booker T. Washington Papers, 1904–1906*, ed. Louis R. Harlan (Urbana: University of Illinois Press, 1979), 115. On plans for Washington's appearance in Carthage, see *CEP*, 20 July 1903, 8; 25 Aug. 1903, 2; 4 Sept. 1903, 6.

27. Sedalia *Weekly Conservator*, 14 Apr. 1905, 2.

hands of Scott and others) reflected major musical elements and important social developments in the age of Booker T. Washington. The very paper and print of Scott's original scores represented a major step up to professional respectability, and James Scott served as an important example to the younger generation.[28]

Scott took an active role in black community affairs, thereby marrying his music to African American ambitions. At the same time that he began his career as a published composer, "Jimmie Scott, the composer of 'A Summer Breeze'" was invited to perform an "original piano solo" to open the spring 1903 commencement exercises at the all-black Lincoln School in the northwest part of town. True to the class motto "Climb, though the rocks be rugged" the one graduate that year—Robert Armstrong—went on to Tuskegee Institute. Something about race relations in southwestern Missouri can be gleaned from the fact that Scott never got to perform as scheduled. The Carthage *Evening Press* explained: "There was disappointment when James Scott, the colored boy composer failed to appear to play his original music, as advertised on the program. He is a shine artist in a barber shop and his employer had declined to let him off."[29]

Three years later, in 1906, while working for C. R. Dumars, a more sympathetic employer, Scott successfully contributed his talents to the school, performing at graduation and responding to demands for an encore. Perhaps he took muted pleasure in the seating arrangement, in which, according to a local reporter, the "balcony and west side of the lower floor will be reserved for the white people for this occasion, while the colored people will occupy the rest of the room." He was still a supporter of the school in 1914, performing to help convince black voters to support a $10,000 bond issue to build a new schoolhouse.[30]

Scott lent his energy and talent to the MSNIA. The association met in Carthage at Chautauqua Park on 11 August 1904, when the Reverend J. W. Watkins, president, and Carthage's Reverend W. B. Long spoke; Boone's and Scott's piano playing at this event did much to bring in an audience. Scott also cooperated closely with the educational efforts of the African Methodist Episcopal Church in Carthage, Joplin, and Neosho, playing a series of concerts of both sacred and secular music to help raise

28. Don Scott, interview with Galen Wilkes, Northridge, Calif., 10 Sept. 1980. This untranscribed taped interview, kindly furnished by Mr. Wilkes, alludes to Douglas Scott, whose activities were reported in *CEP*, 3 May 1906, 4; 18 July 1916, 4; 18 June 1918, 4; 20 June 1918, 3; 12 Sept. 1918, 4.
29. *CEP*, 6 May 1903, 3; 28 July 1903, 2; 25 May 1903, 5 (reporting Hoyt Gierhart's refusal to allow Scott some time off).
30. *CEP*, 2 June 1906, 3; 5 June 1906, 6; 21 Apr. 1914, 3.

money for the church and (as the town newspaper put it) "to educate the colored people up to a better class of music." In 1910 he combined his support for religion and education by playing a Joplin A.M.E. benefit entertainment for Clarence Pierson, who was about to commence his studies at Kansas State University.[31]

The young man from Carthage showed a remarkable versatility, working simultaneously on several projects that strengthened the institutions and morale of black citizens in his own town and in southwestern Missouri. In a burst of activity in 1906–7, Scott helped to organize the Carthage Jubilee Singers, a twenty-five member male chorus, which made its first public appearance at the town opera house on the evening of 31 January 1906. As he had done with his band, Scott selected a vocal quartet from his chorus to perform at the opera house, at courthouse ceremonies, and at various political events.[32]

In addition to devoting his music to black religious and educational institutions, Scott directly applied his wind ensemble to influence state politics. Carthage was a solidly Republican town whose newspaper reminded local blacks at election time that the Republican party was the party of Abraham Lincoln. When, in 1906, state Republican candidates needed black votes to fend off a strong challenge from the Democrats, the paper warned ominously of Democratic plans to repeal the Fifteenth Amendment guaranteeing the civil rights of blacks. A prominent black leader from Joplin, R. H. Hightower, reminded Carthage blacks of "Pitchfork Ben" Tillman's comparison of the Negro to a mule. In response to this threat to the civil rights of his community, Scott called out his marching band to perform for Republican candidates.[33]

Given all his attention to community affairs, Scott decided to settle down in Carthage. His approach was typically deliberate. First, in 1906, he bought a house and lot on the north side of Sixth Street, the second door east of Orchard, for $425. Some idea of the relatively modest dimensions of the house may be gleaned from the $2,500 paid by his employer-patron-publisher C. R. Dumars for an eight-room house that same year. Scott made no mention of any marriage plans; when asked by the local newspaper why he was taking on this responsibility, he responded that he was buying "as an investment."[34]

31. Scott's work for the African Methodist Episcopal Church is documented in *CEP*, 15 Mar. 1906, 2; 19 Mar. 1906, 6; 1 Sept. 1910, 2. Scott's activities in support of the MSNIA are described in *CEP*, 19 July 1904, 5; 11 Aug. 1904, 5; 13 Aug. 1904, 4; 15 Aug. 1904, 4.
32. *CEP*, 27 Jan. 1906, 4; 17 Oct. 1906, 4.
33. *CEP*, 17 Oct. 1906, 4; 1 Nov. 1906, 4; 3 Dec. 1906, 1.
34. *CEP*, 29 Mar. 1906, 3.

Three months later, however, the Carthage *Evening Press* reported that "cards were issued yesterday for the wedding of Jimmie Scott, a talented colored musician who has a position at Dumars music store, and Miss Nora Johnson, a young lady who came here from Springfield. . . . This wedding will be a *recherché* affair in colored circles."[35] Nora Johnson, a vocalist, had sung under Scott's direction in a concert of sacred music at the A.M.E. Church that spring. She took a long eastern trip in August, spending considerable time in Binghamton, New York. The two were quietly married sometime thereafter, the ceremony somehow escaping notice in the papers. The next spring, accompanied by his bride, who retained her maiden name for concert purposes, and by Will McAfee, Scott assisted in a sacred concert presented by Methodists in Neosho.[36]

Scott's published ragtime scores must be interpreted within this context of ambitious craftsmanship, community consciousness, and upward mobility. Before the publication in 1897 of the first ragtime works of William Krell and Tom Turpin, "coon" songs like Ernest Hogan's "All Coons Look Alike to Me" and "My Coal Black Lady" by W. T. Jefferson caricatured blacks in vulgar lyrics sung to lively, syncopated music. Ragtime songs carried on this tradition. Even instrumental rags, such as Joplin's "Original Rags," were sold with racist images on their covers. Plenty of questionable titles were used as well. Scott drew attention to the genre as an instrumental form. Few respectable middle-class white or black pianists would have cared to sing crudely racist lyrics in their living rooms, but such piano rags as Scott's "Grace and Beauty" (1909), packaged in an elegant, racially neutral manner, would have seemed both appropriate and challenging. Their unusual mixture of refinement and syncopated rhythm created a middle ground between the commercialized culture of ragtime songs, sung in Joplin saloons, and the fine art of concert hall music, performed at the yearly concerts of the all-white Calhoun School of Music. Scott's scores reflect the values of middle-class, midwestern African American culture. Fittingly, Scott retained his membership in the Alpha Art Club, an artist's support group and "pillar of Colored Society" in which his wife played a prominent role.[37]

Labels like "ragtime" and "classical music" actually obscure a far more fluid musical reality. James Scott, Scott Joplin, and "Blind" Boone all mixed ragtime with other genres in concert. Boone, swaying constantly

35. *CEP*, 17 July 1906, 3.
36. *CEP*, 15 Apr. 1907, 3.
37. *CEP*, 9 Apr. 1915, 4; 12 Apr. 1917, 3.

at the keyboard, played everything from Liszt's Hungarian Rhapsody No.
6 to Gottschalk's *Last Hope,* from Boone's "Imitation of a Train" and "Rag
Melody No. 1" to "old darky songs." It was reported that, when singing
these songs, Boone "would burst forth into rippling laughter" at the end
of each verse, "keeping such perfect time with the music that the laughter
seemed almost a part of the song." Scott's Jubilee Singers mixed sacred
music with "singing, dancing, specialties, and comedy sketches." Scott
apparently experienced no conflicts in composing old-fashioned waltzes
and popular songs that expressed a different sensibility from the classic
ragtime for which he is best known. It would be a mistake to interpret
classic ragtime in isolation from other related musical forms from which it
sought to be distinguished but could not, at least in public performance,
be entirely removed.[38]

Six of Scott's thirty-eight published works, "Valse Venice" (1909),
"Hearts Longing" (1910), "The Suffragette" (1914), "Springtime of Love"
(1918), "Sweetheart Time" (1909), and "Take Me Out to Lakeside"
(1914), were smoothly professional, accomplished, old-fashioned waltzes.
One of them was published as late as 1918, at the start of the "jazz age."
Multisectional in structure like his rags, the waltzes are organized like
quadrilles, polkas, and marches. They evoke the decorous gentility of Victorian America and mark a conservative position on the spectrum of popular music at the turn of the century. Pre–World War I tastes still included
Victorian nostalgia, which helped to soothe the uneasiness caused in the
parlors of Middle America by reports of urban labor strife, alien radical-
ism, and mass violence. The covers to published editions of Scott's waltzes
suggest refined, often European, reassuring images of rural romantic
bliss.[39]

So, too, the lyrics to Scott's four popular songs catered to exuberant
tastes but avoided tawdry double entendres. "She's My Girl from Anaconda" (1909) celebrates such solid middle-class values as marriage, economic opportunity, and "true blue" monogamous loyalty. The lyrics by
C. R. Dumars cast the alluring "city noise" of New York securely within
a framework of middle-class respectability. The lyrics of "Sweetheart
Time," another old-fashioned song, evoke an idyll of romantic restraint in

38. Boone's concerts are described in *CEP,* 1 June 1907, 4, and in "Reviews of 'Blind' Boone,"
Boone Papers. Scott's Jubilee Singers are described in *CEP,* 27 Jan. 1906, 4.
39. Paul Boyer, *Urban Masses and the Moral Order in America, 1820–1920* (Cambridge: Harvard
University Press, 1978), argues that urbanization functioned as a catalyst for fears about industriali-
zation, immigration, family disruption, religious change, and class divisions. Daniel Walker Howe,
ed., *Victorian America* (Philadelphia: University of Pennsylvania Press, 1976).

which young lovers loyally respect the wishes of the woman's disapproving parents. The cheerful boys and girls in "Take Me Out to Lakeside" seek only clean-cut recreation on Sunday afternoons.

Only the last of Scott's popular songs—"The Shimmie Shake" (1920)—dares to reflect the bawdier world of jazzy popular songs. The hints of black dialect ("I'll 'splain just what I mean . . . Just how this dance do go") and the shivering, quivering, shimmying thrills ("Hey! Hey!") are exceptions to Scott's and John Stark's rule of restrained propriety and point ahead to the more uninhibited world of cabarets, nightclubs, and public or semipublic environments that were to replace the family parlor as the focus of leisure-time entertainment.

Most important, Scott's ragtime scores, which, of course, had no lyrics, created a bright, emotionally antiseptic world of structured fun. As Wilfrid Mellers has put it:

> The essence of the rag is its unremittent rhythmic *pattern* which, though habitually syncopated, is never violent. The melancholy, the frenzy, the ecstasy of the blues are all banished. Instead of lament or orgy, we have a dead-pan manner that shuts out personal sensation. The music is hard, bright, obstinately eupeptic and incorrigibly cheerful; in its machine-made way it is even elegant, like the Negro dandy wearing his straw boater at a raffish angle.[40]

Both the musical characteristics of Scott's works—their diatonic structure and orderly progression toward the reassuring resolution of cadential formulas, their regularized sixteen-bar sections arranged in a fairly predictable order, and their increasing emphasis on keyboard technique—and the prominent patterns in Scott's own life provide evidence of the continuity of Victorian traditions that extended beyond the Victorian era.

When performed with strong rhythmic emphasis at accelerated tempi in commercial surroundings, however, ragtime syncopation did serve to suggest the emotional exuberance of those who had never been assimilated into or who were moving eagerly away from Victorian culture. In the tradition of European charivaris, whose patterns were able both to reinforce and to suggest alternatives to the existing order, Scott's ragtime mixed the genteel with the newer youthful spirit. From 1890 to 1920 the genteel middle class increasingly turned to more "vigorous, exuberant,

---

40. Wilfrid Mellers, *Music in a New Found Land: Themes and Developments in the History of American Music* (New York: Knopf, 1965), 277.

daring, sensual, uninhibited, and irreverent" leisure-time activities. As part of a general upper- and middle-class gravitation toward such forms of working-class mass culture as amusement parks, strenuous sports, dance halls, and saloons, a broad cross section of society "embraced activities which had previously existed only on the margins of American life."[41]

Music played a crucial, if largely unexplored, role in this late nineteenth-century national search for spontaneity, freedom, and vital energy. To many, hard-working regimented bureaucrats and office workers, the mournful, nostalgic popular songs of the 1890s failed to express the thirst for freedom, energetic abandon, and release from an industrial work discipline. According to cultural historian John Higham, older popular songs like Charles K. Harris's "After the Ball" (1892) and Paul Dresser's "My Gal Sal" (1905) projected a drowsy life, "heavy with disappointment and regrets, a life girt with limitations, a life drenched in tears." A more energetic, cheerful, rhythmically vital music expressed more fully the longing for youthful energy and exuberance.[42] Labor historian Roy Rosenzweig describes the search by workers for ways to secure and control "the time and space in which leisure was to be enjoyed." Middle-class midwesterners emulated the many southwestern Missouri miners who had long since learned to relax from the discipline and dangers of the workplace (physical injuries were shockingly common) in saloons, amusement parks, and several forms of physical activity.[43]

The rhythmic piano improvisations of black entertainers like James Scott, Tom Turpin, Artie Matthews, and Louis Chauvin attracted the attention of the youthful middle-class white audience interested in new forms of vernacular dance music. Professional black entertainers discovered an opportunity to further their careers as composers and musicians by performing their syncopated rags in a growing number of commercialized, leisure-time institutions.

Amusement parks such as Lakeside served the recreational needs of

---

41. John Kasson, *Amusing the Million: Coney Island at the Turn of the Century* (New York: Hill and Wang, 1978), 6. On the historical function of charivaris, see Nora Zemon Davis, "The Reasons of Misrule: Youth Groups and Charivaris in Sixteenth-Century France," *Past and Present* 50 (1971): 74.

42. John Higham, "The Reorientation of American Culture in the 1890s," in Higham, *Writing American History: Essays on Modern Scholarship* (Bloomington: Indiana University Press, 1970), 80–82, analyzes the newer, more active sensibilities.

43. Roy Rosenzweig, *Eight Hours for What We Will: Workers and Leisure in an Industrial City, 1870–1920* (Cambridge: Cambridge University Press, 1983), 1, relates workers' leisure-time activities to a struggle for power. Craig Roell, *The Piano in America, 1890–1940* (Chapel Hill: University of North Carolina Press, 1989), 3–28, interweaves the same themes with the history of piano manufacturing.

midwestern towns and small cities. As such they were wholesome, rural, socially conservative versions of the massive, urban, working-class leisure centers such as Chicago's Cheltenham Beach, Riverview, and White City. Lakeside offered a bathing beach, a band pavilion and dance hall, and a vaudeville theater. Attractions like the Forepaugh and Sells traveling circus were staged, and so too dramatic balloon ascensions during which, on occasion, a circus lion and its trainer parachuted separately to earth. Commercial leisure enterprises such as Lakeside Park offered carefully supervised fun and frolic and a temporary suspension of workaday worries. Ragtime contributed to "the illusion of anarchic freedom and heedless release beneath the underlying reality of control." [44]

In performance Scott's music helped to create an atmosphere of wholesome, open-air gaiety, a quality often captured on sheet music covers to his scores. To hold on to his precious job at Lakeside, Scott had to gauge judiciously the level of musical hilarity and irreverence permitted by park managers and community leaders. Lakeside required a conservative approach: alcoholic beverages and gambling were prohibited on the grounds, which were used for baseball games and community picnics. The permissible range of musical emotions was marked at one extreme by Scott's "Take Me Out to Lakeside" and at the other by "Hilarity Rag" (1910), whose cover and agitated, ebullient music expressed a more reckless mood. Scott's leaping, skipping syncopations helped to stimulate the spirit of innocent irreverence so cleverly portrayed by cartoonist Clare Victor Dwiggins on the cover to "Ophelia Rag" (1910).

The cover illustrations for Scott's rags repeat images of the solitary but respectable "New Woman," an elegantly dressed female who has sallied forward from her home to enjoy herself at any one of a number of public places where the new patterns of leisure-time entertainment had been organized. The new women represented on the covers to "The Fascinator" (1903), "Grace and Beauty" (1909), "The Princess Rag" (1911), "Take Me Out to Lakeside," and "Honey Moon Rag" (1916) made statements with their enormous hats. These were a sign, according to historian Kathy Peiss, of liberation from the shawls that immigrant women wore over their heads. (To blacks they would have been signs of liberation from that symbol of slavery and sharecropping, the bandanna.) The voluminous, stylish clothing of the "New Woman" demonstrated a new affluence, public poise, and stunning attire at movies, balls, and entertainments. "Dressing" suggested a glamorous but structured world of dance-floor ro-

---

44. Kasson, *Amusing the Million*, 81.

mance, and many female parlor pianists must have traveled into imaginary
worlds of leisure-time gaiety when playing Scott's rags at home.[45]

When Missourians from Carthage, Joplin, Carterville, Monett, and
Sarcoxie danced to Scott's rags on the hardwood floor of the Lakeside Dance
Pavilion (organizing themselves into the Cajo Dancing Club in 1917),
they probably performed old-time two-steps or modified, refined versions
of the shockingly suggestive "pivoting," "speiling," "tough dances"—the
bunny hug, grizzly bear, turkey trot—that captured the public imagination in big cities like Chicago after 1905. Dumars, for example, chose a
repertoire of two-steps when leading the Light Guard social dance orchestra at Lakeside as late as 1917.[46]

Wherever black entertainers like Scott performed for whites, they
had to come to terms with the expected role and image of the black popular musician. The cover of "A Summer Breeze" includes a small photograph of the young Scott at the beginning of his career, wearing a snugly
fitted jacket, stiff-collared white shirt, and tie. He has perched his derby
hat about as far back on his head as possible. This pose (particularly the
rakishly tilted hat), mildly suggestive of the "Jim Dandy" role established
in minstrelsy, constituted a black popular musician's uniform and a "strat-
egy of attraction," a manipulation of show business forms traditionally
required of black entertainers. Another photograph (see fig. 3) from about
the same period shows a warmer expression, including the hint of a shy
smile.[47]

But blacks in southwestern Missouri continued to re-create many of
the conventions of the minstrel show in their public lives. Carthage's black
Baptist Church ladies' auxiliary arranged a fundraiser in 1910 that featured "Coble and Vernon's 'great colored minstrel.'"[48] In their 1916 Emancipation Day parade, Carthage African Americans organized a procession
of floats. One carrying older residents was labeled "Conditions of 1863";
behind followed a small carriage carrying "Uncle Tom" and "Little Eva"
chased by a pack of bloodhounds. A final float labeled "the slave auction
converted into the school house" proudly displayed schoolchildren from
Carthage. The evening concluded with speeches and a "big cakewalk." The
Emancipation Day celebration at Lakeside Park the following year featured

45. Kathy Peiss, *Cheap Amusements: Working Women and Leisure in Turn-of-the-Century New York* (Philadelphia: Temple University Press, 1986), 63–65.

46. Ibid., 100–101; *CEP*, 26 June 1917, 2.

47. Houston A. Baker, Jr., *Modernism and the Harlem Renaissance* (Chicago: University of Chicago
Press, 1987), 22–30.

48. *CEP*, 21 Sept. 1910, 6.

Figure 3. James Scott, Carthage,
Missouri, ca. 1904.

"Black face comedy in the park theater."[49] It may be that Scott's costume
evoked acceptable show business images among blacks as well as whites.
Social customs may have funneled poor but talented black youngsters like
James Scott into working in barbershops and shoe-shine parlors. As reported in the Carthage *Evening Press,* the "colored porters of the various
barbershops of the city" of Carthage staged a "Big Colored Cakewalk" at
the town Armory in 1915.[50]

In the most frequently reprinted of Scott's early photographs, Scott
adopts an impassive, neutral look, his modest, discreet expression probably a mixture of shyness and nonthreatening neutrality. According to his
cousin Patsy Thomas, Scott, a small man who weighed about 140 pounds,
was diffident and unassuming, preoccupied by his world of music. People
called him the "Little Professor": "He always walked rapidly, looking at
the ground—would pass you on the street and never see you—seemed
always deep in thought. If anyone spoke to him on the street, he would

49. *CEP,* 21 Sept. 1916, 3; 22 Sept. 1916, 4; 7 Aug. 1917, 3.
50. *CEP,* 10 Sept. 1915, 4.

jump, look surprised and pleased. . . . His parting words would always be 'Will you be home tomorrow? O.K. I'll come over and play my new piece for you.'"[51]

While impressed with his fluid mastery of musical notation, even Scott's relatives found him distant and absorbed in thought, usually unwilling to talk about his music. Patsy Thomas remembered him performing, his short fingers dancing over the keyboard, one leg wrapped around the piano stool to keep himself from bounding with the rhythm.[52] Don Scott, James's great-nephew, confirms the impression of a discreet person and adds a revealing insight: "Yea, I've heard several people that knew him. He was a quiet type of man—he loved family—but he was mostly wrapped up in his music. They had a name they called him. They used to call him the Professor, because that is all he wanted to do was to play music and write music and talk music. He was a kidder; he liked to tease, that's what most of the people that I talked to about him remember—mostly as serious about his music and liked to tease people."[53]

The popularity of ragtime faded by the late 1910s, and zinc mining, which had sustained the prosperity of southwestern Missouri, declined abruptly after World War I. Most of Scott's publishing career was already behind him when, by the early 1920s, he moved to Kansas City, Kansas, immediately across the Missouri River from the better-known Kansas City, Missouri. (Since all of the theaters at which Scott is said to have worked were located in Missouri, specific addresses in "Kansas City" will be understood as "Missouri" unless otherwise noted.) In 1922, when his last rag was published, James Scott was listed in the city directory as living at 402 Nebraska Avenue, Kansas City, Kansas. For the next ten years he pursued an active career as a theater musician, bandleader, and arranger.[54]

During his ten professionally active years in Kansas City, Scott continued to affirm his dedication to traditional concert music. He worked at three vaudeville and movie theaters: the Panama Theater at 1709 East Twelfth Street near Woodland, the Lincoln Theatre at Eighteenth and Lydia streets, and the Eblon Theater at 1822 Vine Street. Although Scott's

---

51. As quoted in Blesh and Janis, *They All Played Ragtime*, 115.

52. Ibid.

53. Don Scott, interview with Wilkes, 10 Sept. 1980.

54. Hasse, "Ragtime from the Top," 2; Lawrence Denton, telephone interview with John Hasse, Kansas City, Mo., 28 Dec. 1977. I would like to express my thanks to John Hasse for kindly sharing with me a transcript of this interview, a photocopy of Scott's death certificate, and copies of pages from the Kansas City, Kans., telephone directory. Van Gilder, "James Scott," 142–43, dates Scott's move to Kansas City.

name does not appear in the weekly advertisements of the Kansas City *Call* for those years, Kansas City musicians say that he was among the top professionals in the black music business.

By the time he moved to Kansas City, the black migration from the rural South to the urban North had stimulated a major demand for black musical and theatrical entertainment. Segregation in vaudeville and musicians' unions encouraged the development of various forms of urban entertainment by and for blacks. Scott's generation of black musicians used vaudeville theaters to build careers in the profession.[55]

Vaudeville played an important role in assimilating recent arrivals from the country into city life, "dramatizing the spectrum of humanity in the city" and the diversity of urban life. Audiences were exposed to a variety of human situations, distilled models of everyday behavior, and attitudes toward urban life in the songs, dance numbers, and comedy routines of the vaudeville theater, while they thrilled to the theatrical excitement of acrobatic and animal acts. This democratic form of urban entertainment provided lessons in studied casualness, balance, and poise to rusticated immigrants from the South who enjoyed show business rituals of success, glamour, know-how, and self-confidence. They momentarily escaped from "the dirt, loneliness, and deprivation of present reality."[56]

Pianists played a pivotal role in vaudeville theaters, accompanying a wide variety of acts and silent films with little advance preparation. They also provided musical accompaniment to slide shows and led audience sing-alongs between acts. Many theaters ran two shows per day, opening at noon with a solitary pianist providing all the musical accompaniment. They started over again at 6:00 P.M. with an orchestra, closing at midnight or later. Continuous play catered to women, children, and the unemployed during the day, and to workers at night. For the pianist the vaudeville theater could become a way of life.

Scott, who had played for silent movies in Lakeside Theater, started at the Panama, a small silent-movie house that usually employed only a pianist to accompany its "photoplays." In small theaters like the Panama, the movie features changed frequently, so that the pianist had to be able not only to read the cue sheets supplied with some films but to improvise appropriate sounds for others. This experience encouraged the improvisation and unconventional instrumental sounds soon to be associated with

55. William H. Kenney III, "The Influence of Black Vaudeville on Early Jazz," *The Black Perspective in Music* 14 (1986): 233–48.

56. Albert F. McLean, *American Vaudeville as Ritual* (Lexington: University of Kentucky Press, 1965), 10.

jazz. Keyboard artists had to learn to imitate a startling variety of sounds—including snores, laughter, screams, trains, planes, telegraph keys, steam whistles, and animal noises of all sorts.[57]

A community institution, the Panama offered free admission on Monday, Wednesday, and Friday nights (Thursday was "Theatrical Night," and Saturday was "Souvenir Night"). The management organized special summer picnics for the customers at Liberty Park, where Scott and his cousin Ada Brown, the highly regarded Kansas City blues singer and re-cording artist, performed with the Panama's house band. The newspapers reported that these were happy, feisty, late-night events.[58]

The Panama Theater presented a special week-long series of concerts late in 1922 by the Blind Boone Company including Mme Marguerite Day, the concert soprano with whom Boone often appeared on national tours. Local schoolchildren were brought to these concerts to hear the music of Wollenhaupt, Gottschalk, Verdi, Chopin, Schubert, and Liszt. Boone conceded to popular trends only at the end of these concerts, which he concluded with his own "Marshfield Tornado"—this evoked a "tornado breaking over Marshfield amid the peaceful stillness of a Sabbath morn-ing." Although the craze for female blues singers like Bessie Smith began in 1922, the Panama followed a more traditional musical policy, which Scott encouraged. During the 1920s the city was alive with blues singers and jazz bands, but the Panama all but ignored the trend.[59]

In 1924, when he joined the black musicians' union, Scott moved to the more prominent Lincoln Theatre. Large enough to employ a seven-piece orchestra led by Harry Dillard, the Lincoln had its own vaudeville troupe and also featured the touring acts of the Theater Owners' Booking Association, the most important national booking organization in black vaudeville. In keeping with vaudeville's effort to neutralize the criticisms of moralists and urban reformers, the management at the Lincoln adver-tised a policy of "exceptionally clean, refined" vaudeville, and by 1926 the theater featured an "Augmented Orchestra of 20 Artists" as a regular at-traction. They played specially arranged works between films and vaude-ville shows and, on 13 August 1926, performed "their operatic Selection 'The Light Cavalry.'" Thereafter they were billed as the "Lincoln Sym-phony Orchestra." Lawrence Denton, who worked as a professional musi-cian in Kansas City theaters at the time, recalled that Scott "was the num-

57. Gillian B. Anderson, "The Presentation of Silent Films; or, Music as Anaesthesia," *Journal of Musicology* 5 (1987): 257–95.
58. Kansas City *Call*, 27 July 1923, 8; 9 Jan. 1925, 7.
59. Kansas City *Call*, 1 Dec. 1922, 7; 19 Jan. 1925, 7.

ber one, you know, piano player. Great in classics . . . concertos . . . like
[Liszt's] Second Hungarian Rhapsody." Denton felt that Scott was particularly valuable in playing the special arranged accompaniments that arrived at the theaters with the more elaborate new films.[60]

This interest in concert music typified musical activities in the larger
urban black theaters across the country from about 1910 to 1928. In Chicago, for example, Dave Peyton, Erskine Tate, and Clarence Jones
pioneered in organizing large theater orchestras that emphasized sight
reading and precision section work for a wide variety of orchestral compositions. As in Chicago, so too in Kansas City there were two musical
camps: the orchestral musicians and the cabaret improvisers. By 1926
Bennie Moten (1894–1935) was building a big band at the Paseo Dance
Hall at the corner of Eighteenth Street and Paseo. Moten, the best-
publicized maker of jazz and dance music in Kansas City, bought full-page
advertisements in the Call and staged dramatic battles of the bands. Ada
Brown sang with Moten's orchestra, but Scott, like so many other black
musicians, doggedly pursued a more conservative approach to music
making.[61]

Between 1926 and 1928 Scott worked at the Eblon Theater, which
had opened in the fall of 1923. The Eblon was billed as "The ONLY Theater Owned by a Negro in Greater Kansas City," and owner Homer "Jap"
Eblon proudly advertised that "The Music Alone Is Well Worth the Price."
The theater was in the middle of Kansas City's entertainment district,
across the street from the Booker T. Washington Hotel and a few steps
from Jones Pool Hall, the Lincoln Dance Hall, the Subway Club, and
Piney Brown's Club. Scott played in "Goopy" Taylor's Eblon orchestra,
which included Baby Lovett, drums, Homer Franklin, trombone, Epps
Jackson, bass horn, Walter Brown, trumpet, Taylor, leader and violin,
and Chick Irvin, saxophone. In November 1928 Eblon replaced the band
with "a genuine Wicks pipe organ . . . which sets the purchaser
back $15,000." Scott manipulated the fifty-two stops on this instrument
before sound films drove him out of business about 1930. The young,
scuffling Count Basie and his friends sneaked into the Eblon to play on
the Wicks, too.[62]

60. Denton, telephone interview with Hasse, 28 Dec. 1977; Kansas City Call, 29 Sept. 1922, 7.
61. Kansas City Call, 8 Dec. 1922, 7; 7 Dec. 1923, 6; 13 Aug. 1926, 5; 24 Sept. 1926, 6.
Thomas J. Hennessey, "The Black Chicago Establishment, 1919–1930," Journal of Jazz Studies 2
(1974): 15–45.
62. Denton, telephone interview with Hasse, 28 Dec. 1977; Kansas City Call, 12 Oct. 1923, 7; 26
Oct. 1923, 4–5; 18 Jan. 1924, 6; 24 Feb. 1928, 5. William "Count" Basie with Albert Murray,
Good Morning Blues: The Autobiography of Count Basie (New York: Random House, 1985), 14–16.

Figure 4. Advertisement for Lincoln Theatre, Kansas City *Call*, 13 August 1926.

Scott's last ten years were not easy. Like so many other black musicians who had built professional careers in the movie houses, he suffered with the arrival of movie sound tracks. Moreover, his wife, Nora, died at about the time he lost his theater work. Scott persevered, giving music lessons and leading an eight-piece band that played for parties and special occasions. He is said to have continued to compose, but no manuscripts have survived apart from several arrangements of popular tunes written by Paul Banks, Hattie Pearson, and Ida Mae Banks.[63] Scott moved frequently during his last eight years. Shortly before the end of his life, he took up residence in the home of his cousin Ruth Callahan, at 1926 Springfield Street in Kansas City, Kansas. He died of kidney failure and hardening of the arteries in Douglas Hospital on 30 August 1938 and was buried in Westlawn Cemetery beside his wife. For many years his unmarked grave site was a dumping ground, but research and campaigning by Smiley and

---

63. The following manuscripts carry the legend "Arr. by James [or "Jimmie"] Scott" and were written by Paul Banks and Hattie Pearson: "Chattanooga Blues," 25 Oct. 1923; "Skeezix," 10 Oct. 1923; "Safety First Blues"; "Sugar Daddy Blues," 1 Oct. 1924; and "Broadway Belles," 1 July 1924. The following was written by the above plus Ida Mae Banks: "Tut Ankh Amen's Dream." Uncataloged music, Music Division, Library of Congress.

Figure 5. Eblon Theater Orchestra, ca. 1924. *Left to right:* Baby
Lovett, drums; Homer Franklin,
trombone; Eppi Jackson, bass
horn; Walter Brown, trumpet;
Guile ("Goopy") Taylor, leader/
violin; James Scott, piano; and
Chick Irvin, saxophones. Photo
courtesy of Duncan Schiedt.

Helen Wallace led the Maple Leaf Club to purchase and dedicate a head-
stone in 1981.[64]

Although Scott died in urban anonymity, the small-town Carthage
citizen had made a sizable contribution to the professional and artistic
aspirations of African American musicians. His challenging piano works
enriched a core literature that distinguished classic ragtime from the easy
commercialism of ragtime songs, creating a purely instrumental medium
meant for playing and listening. His keyboard abilities, written into his
later rags in particular, became the emblem of his drive toward a musically
challenging form of black popular music.

Observers of black vernacular music did not miss Scott's importance.
Orchestra leader and columnist Dave Peyton, a champion of musical literacy, traced "The Origin of Jazz" for the Chicago *Defender* in 1925. He
placed James Scott in a line running from Scott Joplin through Will Mar-
ion Cook and J. Rosamond Johnson to James Reese Europe, C. Luckeyth
Roberts, Maceo Pinkard, Clarence Williams, and Joe Jordan, practitioners
of formally notated black popular music.[65]

James Scott's ragtime and the concept of classic ragtime together
document the fluidity behind the labels historians attach to musical styles.

64. Scott, Certificate of Death, copy kindly furnished by John Hasse. Kansas City *Times*, 23 Jan.
1978, sec. 4A.
65. Dave Peyton, "The Origin of Jazz," Chicago *Defender*, 12 Dec. 1925, 7.

Scott's rags, rooted in African American culture, also reflect the turn-of-the-century world of popular leisure-time merriment, as well as a mixture of late Victorian gentility and the ambitions of the new black middle class. This original synthesis both reinforced the existing social order and suggested alternatives to it. It expressed a surging new democratic sensibility but also included major characteristics of traditional nineteenth-century piano music. It marked the distinctive sound of the ragtime era and can remind us that ragtime was not (quite yet) jazz.

THE MUSIC OF JAMES SCOTT

Scott DeVeaux

THE MUSIC PRESENTED IN THIS EDITION—thirty rags, four waltzes, and four songs by James Scott—constitutes one of the richest and most fully developed repertories of the ragtime era.[1] The rags are often cited as exemplars of "classic ragtime," the phrase coined by St. Louis publisher John Stark to describe the type of ragtime composition featured in his catalog. A more precise definition of classic ragtime has yet to be found, and modern scholars continue to debate how widely the term should be applied. But by even the most narrow criteria of time, place, and personal association, Scott qualifies. He was a midwesterner, spending his entire career in the state of Missouri. Most of his music was published by Stark's firm. And perhaps most important, his music exemplifies the general sense of "classic": of the highest rank in its genre, and possessed of lasting value.

---

1. The enumeration of pieces by James Scott does not include the reconstruction of "Calliope Rag," which does not appear in this edition. See Editorial Policy, under "Sources."

EARLY INFLUENCES AND
MUSICAL DEVELOPMENT

The earliest of Scott's piano pieces are juvenilia, published when the young pianist was barely eighteen. Compared with the early works of Scott Joplin, they are remarkably idiomatic and self-assured. But then, by 1903, Scott had the published example of Joplin and other ragtime composers to follow. Joplin's "Maple Leaf Rag" had appeared in 1899. Its broad success proved that it was possible for a ragtime composer to reach a large audience without being restricted to the simple harmonic and rhythmic conventions of the day.[2] Within the next few years, other works by Joplin were published, the beginnings of a rich, idiosyncratic repertory that showed the unexpected directions in which ragtime might lead.

Through his work as a demonstration pianist in Charles Dumars's music store, Scott encountered a wide range of ragtime compositions. It is apparent that he kept up with the most recent efforts of ragtime composers, especially Joplin and Kansas City native Charles L. Johnson, since published rags by these composers formed the basis for his earliest efforts at composition. Thinly veiled borrowings from Joplin and Johnson may be found throughout the three early pieces published by Dumars in 1903 and 1904. The fourth or "D" strain of his earliest published piece, "A Summer Breeze" (1903), for example, is nearly identical to the second strain of Joplin's "Elite Syncopations," published in the previous year.

Joplin's "Breeze from Alabama" (1902) is another piece that Scott seems to have studied closely. Its introduction was the obvious inspiration for the opening measures (and perhaps the title) of Scott's "Summer Breeze." Its opening strain provided the main motivic material for the first strain of "The Fascinator." Even its unusual key scheme, which places the trio in the flatted submediant instead of the customary subdominant, is imitated in "The Fascinator" (a modulation from C major to A-flat major in both cases). Similarly, a simple but effective transitional passage in the first strain of "The Fascinator" (A:7–8; "A" refers to the first or A strain, "7–8" to the measure numbers within the strain—see Editorial Policy, under "Terminology") may be traced back to the corresponding passage in Charles L. Johnson's "'Doc' Brown's Cake Walk" of 1899. Such ingenuous borrowings may be readily forgiven as the unorthodox means by which Scott mastered the basic manner of ragtime composition. Fortunately, he chose his models well and learned quickly.

With his fourth published rag, "Frog Legs Rag" (1906), Scott had begun to discover his own style—a buoyant and vigorously rhythmic

2. Edward A. Berlin, *Ragtime: A Musical and Cultural History* (Berkeley and Los Angeles: University of California Press, 1980), 81ff.

piano technique wedded to a superbly crafted and carefully controlled harmonic idiom. "Frog Legs" was the first of Scott's rags to be published by John Stark and was probably his most popular work (subsequent publications routinely identified Scott as "composer of 'Frog Legs Rag'"). It is a brilliant and fully developed piece of music and a good place to begin examining Scott's distinctive stylistic traits.

From the outset of "Frog Legs Rag," the influence of Joplin, especially the extroverted Joplin of the "Maple Leaf Rag," is clear. There is the emphatic, unadorned opening (the first of Scott's rags without an introduction): a pair of octaves leading immediately, as with the "Maple Leaf," to paired two-measure phrases moving from tonic to dominant. The second strain likewise emulates the harmonic structure and the characteristic piano figuration of its counterpart in the "Maple Leaf." In the trio the melodic writing recalls a Joplin style of a different kind—the sinuous, chromatic single-note melodic lines of, for example, the B strain of "Easy Winners" (1901).

Still, the style is distinctly Scott's own. The listener is apt to be struck first by its pianistic brilliance. As difficult as the "Maple Leaf Rag" is to play, "Frog Legs Rag" is harder still, if only because its figurations require so much agility. Arpeggios spanning two octaves (A:5–7), rapid octave passagework (C:6–7), and wide leaps (D:1–4), found only in the most athletic of Joplin's compositions, are part of Scott's ordinary vocabulary. But the technique is not merely for display. The most challenging passages are integrated into the overall plan, in some cases embodying the basic thematic material. The exuberant octave leaps in the final strain that provide a satisfying close to the rag as a whole, for example, establish a kind of call-and-response pattern that was to become a Scott trademark.

The listener is also likely to be struck by a sense of unity. This, too, is a Scott trademark: an economy of means arising from the persistent use of a few distinct musical ideas. The first two measures of "Frog Legs Rag" provide the basic thematic material for virtually the entire A strain. Insistent repetition builds up a tension that is relieved first by the sweeping arpeggio in measures 6–7 and finally by the drive to the cadence in measures 14–16. The distinctive phrase structure of the opening of this strain, falling into the pattern of 2 + 2 + 4 bars, appears again in the trio. Similar correspondences may be found in the harmonic progressions: those of the A and C strains are closely related, while the B and D strains are nearly identical.

In lesser hands such economy of means might be wearying. But the variety of pianistic textures and a fine attention to detail prevent repetition from lapsing into monotony. One need only compare the closing measures of the C and D strains—based on the same melodic and harmonic outline, but subtly differentiated—to see how Scott achieves variety in unity. Repetition reinforces the tendency of Scott's music toward a certain brittle cheerfulness, perhaps, but it also helps to impart a solidity and a driving momentum that are among the music's best characteristics.

Less than three years later, Scott published "Grace and Beauty" (1909). If "Frog Legs Rag" is Scott's finest Joplinesque composition, "Grace and Beauty" completes the transition to an individual style. The strengths of "Frog Legs" are still evident: a clearheaded economy of means, an uncommonly demanding piano technique, and an unrelenting rhythmic drive. To these may be added new traits that show the flowering of Scott's compositional skills: a sure-handed control of chromatic voice leading and, above all, a careful balancing of different pianistic textures.

The variety and fullness of textures is the most striking aspect of "Grace and Beauty": the sweeping pentatonic ascents of the opening strain are followed by the punchy octaves of the B strain, the delicate broken-chord filigree of the trio, and the powerful syncopated chords of the concluding section. Few of Scott's contemporaries explored the piano keyboard with such confidence. Fewer still combined such fluid and idiomatic passagework with as sophisticated and subtle a use of chromatic harmony and motivic manipulation.

The last strain of "Grace and Beauty" may be taken as an example. Within this rousing, straightforward climax to the piece are many characteristic details that reveal the composer's craft. The main melodic motive of the opening measures, the B♭–A♭ appoggiatura in the right-hand offbeat chords, is subtly echoed in the bass line of measure 2, where it is part of a passing motion (the dissonant B♭ resolving to A♭ on the subsequent beat). Another detail particularly characteristic of Scott is the rich sonority of the left-hand writing in measure 8, where he breaks away from the usual octave texture to establish a tenor voice moving in parallel motion to the descending chords in the right hand. Nor should one overlook the intricate series of chromatic passing chords in the climactic final phrase, moving in measures 14–15 to a melodic peak on A♭ and B♭—the same two notes that figured so prominently at the beginning of the strain. All these details combine with the generally extroverted idiom to create a musical style at once ingenuous and technically accomplished.

The distance that Scott traveled in the space of three years from the relative crudities of the Dumars rags to the sophistication of "Frog Legs Rag" is remarkable. If the further path of his development is not always evident from the succession of rags in this edition, that is because they were not necessarily published in the order of composition. Publishers may have held manuscripts in backlogs for years until it was convenient to publish them.[3] In the absence of surviving manuscripts, a precise chronology for Scott's music seems impossible. (In this edition the pieces have been ordered within genre by date of publication. If more than one work was published in a given year, they are presented in alphabetical order—except for Scott's two earliest rags, "A Summer Breeze" and "The Fascinator.") But internal stylistic evidence suggests that some rags may not have been published until years following their composition.

A number of rags published after 1906—"Kansas City Rag" (1907), "Sunburst Rag" (1909), "Great Scott Rag" (1909), "Ophelia Rag" (1910), "The Princess Rag" (1911), and "Evergreen Rag" (1915)—have a certain stylistic affinity with the three Dumars rags. The pianistic texture tends to be thinner and less varied in these pieces. In place of the dense three- and four-note chords and rapid registral shifts characteristic of such contemporaneous rags as "Grace and Beauty" (1909), "Hilarity Rag" (1910), and "Ragtime Oriole" (1911), one finds a more straightforward exposition of melodic material, usually in unadorned octaves and thirds and sixths. A further link with the Dumars rags is the persistence of Scott's youthful habit of borrowing from the work of other composers, especially Charles L. Johnson. "Great Scott Rag" takes its opening two-measure phrase directly from the 1899 Johnson composition "Scandalous Thompson."[4] Similarly, the A strain of "Ophelia Rag" reworks important material (the opening motive, the harmonic movement from I to VI, and the chromatic run in measures 7–8) originally found in the trio of Johnson's "'Doc' Brown's Cake Walk," also published in 1899.

Why would these pieces not have been published in order of composition? One explanation might be that Scott came to Stark in 1906 with a number of pieces already composed. Having decided to take a chance with the young composer, Stark would have singled out the most promising of the available pieces for publication, the first of which was "Frog Legs Rag." (The strong resemblance of "Frog Legs" to the most successful composition in the Stark catalog, Joplin's "Maple Leaf Rag," would have been a selling point for Stark.) Once "Frog Legs" proved its worth in the marketplace, Stark would then have published material from the remainder of Scott's compositions, interspersing new rags like "Grace and Beauty" with ear-

---

3. Stark, for example, published three Joplin rags ("Felicity Rag," "Kismet Rag," and "Reflection Rag") long after his relationship with Joplin had been severed in 1909.

4. Bob Wright and Trebor Tichenor, "James Scott and C. L. Johnson: An Unlikely Musical Kinship," *Rag Times* 6 (1972): 4.

lier, technically less adept pieces. (Scott, of course, felt free to take his compositions elsewhere, publishing "Great Scott Rag" with the Allen Music Company of Columbia, Missouri, in 1909.) Some of the pieces may in fact be combinations of old and new material. The trio to "Ophelia Rag," for example, displays a full-voiced, varied texture with dense octave passagework and an independent tenor voice that contrasts markedly with the relatively simple texture of the opening strain. Perhaps "Ophelia" was an earlier composition spruced up for publication in 1910 through the interpolation of a freshly composed trio.

The older style rags largely disappear after 1911—although Scott's last rag, "Broadway Rag" (1922), is a throwback, resembling "Great Scott Rag" and "Sunburst Rag" more than the densely scored pieces of the late teens and twenties. It seems likely that the pieces published during Scott's most productive decade, the 1910s, appeared more or less in the order in which they were written. There are important innovations in these pieces: the use of the minor mode in "Rag Sentimental" (1918) and "Pegasus" (1920); the exquisite lyricism of "Troubadour Rag" (1919) and "Modesty Rag" (1920); and above all, the denser, aggressively virtuosic piano style found in "Efficiency Rag" (1917), "Peace and Plenty Rag" (1919), and other late pieces. In general, a tendency toward complexity and density in Scott's writing parallels the chronological progression of publications and seems a genuine development in his style.

For all this the unity of Scott's oeuvre is more striking than its diversity. Scott for the most part stayed within the stylistic boundaries established well before 1910, contenting himself with intricate and sophisticated variations on familiar formulas. In this he contrasts most sharply with Joplin. Throughout his career the elder composer searched restlessly for variety and novelty in his harmonic forms and unexpected twists in the details of his melodic writing. The ultimate expression of this is Joplin's extraordinary "Euphonic Sounds," with its restrained pianistic textures and startling harmonic shifts. But even the "Maple Leaf Rag," the most popular rag ever published, derives much of its effect from an unusually complex and asymmetric harmonic scheme. Joplin's refusal to be content with the easily grasped and the easily achieved gives his music its startling originality. It is also the source of the frustrating incompleteness of Joplin's later career, his reluctance to continue to pour his energies into ragtime and his quixotic foray into opera where he was ill-equipped—if not by talent, then surely by resources—to go.

Scott, who preferred consistency to contrast, and variation to innovation, showed no such restlessness. There is a satisfying sense of completeness and fulfillment to his life's work. It is a body of music in which the pieces all bear a family resemblance. If this means that the lesser passages have a tendency toward sameness, it is also true that his best pieces display an organic unity that has no rival in the ragtime repertory.

RHYTHM   Nowhere is the tendency toward internal consistency more evident than with rhythm. Rhythmic contrast through syncopation is, of course, ragtime's defining trait, as well as its vital link to the African American folk tradition. The steady alternation of bass notes and middle-register chords in the pianist's left hand (sometimes called "boom-chick," after its sound, and later dubbed "stride," after its visual appearance) produces an insistent, dancelike pulse. Within this steady $\frac{2}{4}$ meter, the right hand plays strong contrasting accents falling on the normally unaccented, or "weak," beats of the measure. Certain pianistic figurations in the right hand, especially the alternation of single notes with chords or octaves (as in the second strain of "Frog Legs Rag"), lend themselves naturally to this purpose. The listener is left with the impression of two interrelated, but distinct, layers: an unvarying rhythmic foundation in the left hand and a shifting web of cross-rhythms in the right.

The earliest rags relied on a relatively mild form of rhythmic contrast: the "cakewalk" figure and its augmentation (see ex. 1).[5] By the time that James Scott began to compose, this rhythmic style was already on the decline. Aside from "On the Pike," only "The Princess Rag" and "Evergreen Rag" (in its trio) use these old-fashioned devices consistently—further evidence for their earlier date of composition.[6] All other rags use the more flexible form of syncopation, with ties arching across the two beats of the measure.

Example 1. The cakewalk figure

Underlying the surface variety of Scott's syncopation is the consistent, often unrelenting, use of a handful of basic rhythmic patterns. The most common of these by far is defined by a syncopated accent on the fourth sixteenth note of the measure, suggesting (assuming a subdivision of the $\frac{2}{4}$ measure into eight sixteenth notes) the additive pattern 3 + 3 +

5. Berlin, *Ragtime*, 82–88.
6. It should be noted, however, that the augmented cakewalk rhythm is used for occasional contrast in a number of later rags, particularly "Efficiency Rag" and "Peace and Plenty Rag."

2 against the even two-beat pulse (see ex. 2). This rhythmic pattern was not unique to Scott. It is a staple of the African American folk tradition and is ultimately traceable to Caribbean and West African music. In the 1920s a condensed version of the pattern (lacking the final eighth note) surfaced as the Charleston. It is a pervasive presence in Scott's music, even where not immediately evident in the notation. Underlying the more rapid surface movement of the melodic line in the opening strain of "Grace and Beauty," for example, is an inner voice that emphasizes the 3 + 3 + 2 grouping (see ex. 3).

Example 2. Additive 3 + 3 + 2 syncopation

3   +   3   +   2

Example 3. James Scott, "Grace and Beauty," A1:2–3

It is not unusual to find this rhythmic pattern used as the basis for entire strains, not to say entire pieces. Once again, "Frog Legs Rag" provides an example. Of its eighty-four measures (excluding repeats), sixty-six have syncopated rhythms in the right-hand part. Of these, sixty—over 90 percent—may be reduced to rhythmic patterns with a prominent accent on the fourth sixteenth note (see table 1). One of the few exceptions—the rhythm of B:4 and 6—may be understood as a syncopated anacrusis, extending the additive 3 + 3 + 2 pattern back into the previous measure (see ex. 4). The same category of rhythmic patterns would account for nearly all of the measures in the next published rag, "Kansas City Rag"—and for many other rags as well.

The B strain of "Grace and Beauty" introduces a related, but distinct, rhythmic motive with syncopated accents on the second as well as the fourth sixteenth (see ex. 5). Again, emphasis through repetition is the basic technique. The pattern not only pervades the B strain but works its way into the C strain as well. Such repetition is often thoroughgoing, and in a few pieces it verges on the monotonous. In the trio of "Prosperity

Rag," for example, the opening rhythmic motive (see ex. 6) is heard in thirteen of its sixteen measures. The most extreme case is "Honey Moon Rag," where the figure (ex. 7), often emphasized by heavy, full chords, is heard in every strain and connecting passage—72 out of 136 measures (with repeats).

Table 1. Syncopated Right-Hand Rhythmic Patterns in "Frog Legs Rag"

Pattern	Number of measures
	20
	16
	12
	9
	3

Example 4. James Scott, "Frog Legs Rag," B:4–5

$$3 + 3 + 3 + 2$$

Example 5. James Scott, "Grace and Beauty," B:1–2

Example 6. James Scott, "Prosperity Rag," C:1–2

Example 7. James Scott, "Honey Moon Rag," B2:1

Still another rhythmic pattern frequently used by Scott may more properly be called "polymetric"—with the sixteenth-note pulse grouped in threes against the steady $\frac{2}{4}$ foundation. (This particular rhythmic device is often referred to—confusingly—as "secondary rag.")[7] In Scott's music the metrical grouping of three is almost always established by an unequal pair of notes, a sixteenth followed by an eighth (ex. 8). Typically, this pattern is reserved for final strains, where its polyrhythmic momentum makes for a rousing conclusion (see, for example, "Ragtime Oriole," "Paramount Rag," and "Rag Sentimental"). But in the cascades of broken octaves of "Hilarity Rag," it serves as a powerful opening statement as well.

Example 8. Scott's polymetric pattern

All of these rhythmic patterns, to be sure, are basic to ragtime and turn up with great frequency in the work of all ragtime composers. But the consistency with which Scott relies on one or two such patterns in the course of a piece is remarkable, particularly in view of the variety found in other dimensions of his craft. Rhythmic consistency is one of the defining characteristics of his style, and it is one of the important ways in which he diverges from Joplin.[8]

To see how different was Joplin's approach, one has only to look at any representative rag. Joplin is almost fastidious in his concern for rhythmic variety and rarely sustains a given syncopated pattern for more than a few measures before countering it with a contrasting pattern or with unsyncopated material. (Scott also uses unsyncopated passages, but they tend to be neutral, undifferentiated strings of sixteenth notes; Joplin's usually have a clearly defined rhythmic shape that serves as an effective contrast to syncopated material.) The constantly shifting rhythm of Joplin's pieces imposes a moderate tempo on the performer and makes Joplin seem like a nineteenth-century composer using "folk" polyrhythmic material in a styl-

---

7. "Secondary rag" is confusing because the corresponding term "primary rag" (covering, presumably, all other forms of syncopation) is never used. The concept of polymeter, in any case, is found throughout all African American music. Referring to it as "secondary rag" implies that its use in ragtime is a special case, which it is not.

8. Curiously, the additive pattern prominently featured in Joplin's "Maple Leaf"—a polymetric grouping of sixteenth notes in threes, but beginning with an eighth rest—is conspicuous in its absence from most of Scott's rags. The exceptions are "The Fascinator" (D strain), "Ophelia Rag" (B strain), and "Ragtime Oriole" (C strain).

ized, if elegant way. Conversely, the rhythmic insistency of Scott's rags strongly suggests a brisker, more vigorous, and more percussive style of performance, foreshadowing the jazz-based dance music to come in the decades ahead.

HARMONY   If Scott's use of rhythm draws on the African American folk tradition, his use of harmony is best understood as a sophisticated extension of the common practice of vernacular music at the turn of the century. The basic idiom may be heard in his parlor waltzes, charming pieces that despite their lack of ragtime syncopation demonstrate Scott's skills to good advantage. Harmony in the waltzes is firmly tonal and essentially diatonic, albeit enriched by chains of secondary dominants, chromatic passing motion, and the diminished seventh chord. Dissonances tend to be mild: neighbor motions, passing tones, and appoggiaturas resolve neatly to chord tones; sixths, sevenths, and ninths added to tonic and dominant chords are often left unresolved.

As in the rags, the animating force behind the best passages in the waltzes is a clear voice leading that makes the progression from chord to chord convincing, never arbitrary. Even where passagework seems to dominate (as in the opening strain of "The Suffragette"), the integrity of the inner voices is carefully preserved. The music is always melodic, even if not explicitly tuneful. Bass lines in particular emerge from the conventional left-hand accompanimental patterns to play a particularly active and independent melodic role. In the trios of both "Valse Venice" and "The Suffragette," soprano and bass form a kind of two-voice counterpoint, leading to a logical and graceful shading of root position and inversion chords.

In the more vigorous ragtime pieces, the bass line assumes even greater importance. The trombone imitations in "On the Pike" (B:1–4) may be dismissed as a coloristic device, but as early as "Kansas City Rag" (A:1–7), Scott discovered how much an independent bass line contributed not only to variety in the harmony but to an overall sense of drive and forward momentum. The bass is always active, breaking away from the "boom-chick" figure long enough to stride purposefully in steady eighth notes, even in harmonically static passages. Many of the most interesting harmonies are developed in this manner. A case in point is the striking opening of "Efficiency Rag," which may again be thought of as a two-part counterpoint between the leaping soprano melody and the chromatically descending bass. Each chord in the opening three measures is in inversion—including, in the space of a measure and a half, no fewer than *three* different third inversion dominant sevenths. So restlessly moving is the bass line in the first strain proper that one does not encounter a root position tonic triad until the ninth measure—a remarkable occurrence for a music as solidly tonal as ragtime.

With time Scott's command of chromatic harmony grew steadily more sophisticated. Even in his earliest efforts Scott demonstrated a working familiarity with the staple of nineteenth-century harmony, the diminished seventh. At first the novice composer used this highly unstable chord only in the simplest of contexts, resolving forcefully either to V⁷ ("The Fascinator," A:6–7) or to I⁶₄ ("A Summer Breeze," A:14–15). But in the mature rags one finds a freer and more inventive use of the diminished seventh as a coloristic device, adding tension or variety to the thematic material. Diminished chords are often highlighted by vigorous or particularly fanciful figurations, as in the syncopated broken octaves of "Hilarity Rag" (B:13) or the cascading introduction to "Ragtime Oriole." In "Climax Rag" Scott actually begins the opening strain with two measures worth of diminished seventh chords. (The effect is less dramatic than one might expect, since the chord is an embellishment of the tonic triad that resolves easily into the prevailing tonal framework.) In a few of the later rags, the inherent ambiguity of the diminished seventh—or, more accurately, a succession of diminished sevenths—is skillfully exploited to create a tension that momentarily stretches the boundaries of tonality. This happens noisily in the B strain of "Pegasus" and with grace and panache in one of Scott's most brilliant and imaginative passages, the trio to "New Era Rag."

Surprisingly, Scott almost never used the ♭VI chord, the stock-in-trade of the concert march and a particular favorite of Joplin's. (The sole exception is the trio of the late rag "Peace and Plenty," which is also unique in using an extended interlude, or "dogfight," in between repetitions of the trio.) He seemed in general to prefer gentler, less unstable forms of dissonance, such as the half-diminished chord, which provides the distinctive coloring to the opening strain of "Ragtime Oriole" and "Victory Rag," among others.

In the later rags especially, a characteristically rich sound arises from the freer and more expressive use of ninths and sixths attached to tonic and dominant chords. The effect may be bright and jangling, as in the percussive chords of the B strain to "New Era Rag" and the dissonant clusters of "Don't Jazz Me—Rag" (B:4, 6, 8, 12), or exquisitely lyrical, as in "Modesty Rag" and "Troubadour Rag." Scott's penchant for luxurious chromaticism reaches its peak in the latter two pieces, which rank among the loveliest rags ever written. The opening measures of the B strain of "Modesty

Rag" combine chromatic passing tones and expressive appoggiaturas with an unusually rich array of seventh and ninth chords. So intricate is the unfolding of the harmony in this and other passages in "Modesty Rag," "Troubadour Rag," and "Rag Sentimental" that a slower, more leisurely tempo than the usual seems to be called for.

HARMONIC STRUCTURE

Harmonic structure in Scott's instrumental music is inextricably wedded to form. As is typical of music designed for or derived from the dance, the impulse in ragtime is toward symmetric designs based on the four-bar phrase. Four such phrases are combined into the closed sixteen-bar section, or "strain." By the time Scott began working out the harmonic structures for his own rags, certain conventions, derived in large part from the march, were already widely accepted.

A typical pattern for a sixteen-bar strain is aa'—two eight-bar periods (usually further subdivided into a pair of four-bar phrases), beginning with identical material and differing at their cadences. For the most part, harmonies tend to be simple, sticking close to tonic and dominant. But at measure 13 of the sixteen-bar form, the harmonic rhythm often quickens in preparation for the cadence marking the end of the strain. Here the composer uses relatively elaborate means—circle-of-fifths motion, chromatic harmonies (diminished chords, ♭VI chords)—to highlight the arrival at the cadential formula I⁶₄–V⁷–I (these devices have been collectively referred to by Edward Berlin as "measure 13 conventions").[9]

Although the individual strains in Scott's rags differ widely in detail, certain underlying patterns are easy to discern. In the most frequently used of these patterns, the first three four-bar phrases are identical: two measures of the dominant (characteristically in second inversion) followed by two measures of the tonic. The remaining phrase consists of "measure 13 conventions" driving toward the final cadence (see fig. 6). The obvious immediate precedent for this practice is the second strain of Joplin's "Maple Leaf Rag." But it is a formula basic not only to ragtime but also to the march: well-known examples in the Sousa repertory include the B strains of "The Washington Post" and "Manhattan Beach," and the opening and closing strains of "Semper Fidelis." Beginning with "Frog Legs Rag," few of Scott's rags are without it; and in one case all three strains of a rag ("Quality") are based on it.

If the listener senses an underlying similarity from strain to strain

9. Berlin, *Ragtime*, 94–95, 140.

Figure 6. Typical sixteen-bar harmonic progression

m. 1

| V$^4_3$ | | % | I | | % | |

m. 5

| V$^4_3$ | | % | I | | % | |

m. 9

| V$^4_3$ | | % | I | | % | |

m. 13

| measure 13 ┆ conventions | I$^6_4$ – V | I | |

and from rag to rag in Scott's music, it is likely to stem from the pervasiveness of this harmonic structure. The constant oscillation between dominant and tonic not only establishes the harmonic rhythm but predisposes Scott to certain thematic material. In traditional harmony the only melodic note that can be supported by both the dominant and tonic harmonies is the fifth degree of the scale. But with the sort of mild dissonance much favored in the period, the sixth degree of the scale may be used as well, forming the harmonies of a dominant ninth and a tonic sixth, respectively (see ex. 9). Composer after composer in the late nineteenth century exploited these pleasantly piquant sounds. One has only to think of the opening phrases of Strauss's "Blue Danube Waltz"—or, closer to home, the B strain of "The Washington Post"—to see how widespread is the gesture of two paired melodic phrases, with a dissonant sixth degree supported first by dominant and then by tonic harmonies. With Scott this musical idea becomes an ingrained habit, suited to his liking for short, paired phrases (see ex. 10). To the end of his career, he delighted in offering new variations on this time-honored device, occasionally clustering the fifth and sixth degrees in the same chord (as in "Hilarity Rag"; see ex. 10b).

Example 9. Harmonies of dominant ninth and tonic sixth

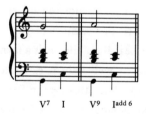

V^7 I   V^9 Iadd 6

One useful variant of the basic structure was inspired by the trio of Joplin's "Maple Leaf Rag": the third phrase, instead of continuing the dominant–tonic movement, moves instead to the supertonic (ii). Several passages in Scott's late compositions are modeled on this strain: the A strain of "New Era Rag," the trios of "Victory Rag" and "Efficiency Rag."

Example 10. Scott's use of paired melodic phrases with a dissonant sixth degree supported first by dominant then by tonic harmonies

a. "Climax Rag," B:1–4

b. "Hilarity Rag," D:1–4

c. "Victory Rag," B:5–8

d. "Ophelia Rag," B:5–8

e. "Troubadour Rag," B:5–8

The distinctive chord clusters of the "Maple Leaf" trio inspired still other strains (the trios of "Ragtime Oriole" and "Quality"). Indeed, the "Maple Leaf" continued to cast a long shadow over Scott's repertory. A number of rags echo in their first strains the distinctive opening of the "Maple Leaf": a pair of identical two-bar phrases moving from tonic to dominant, often introduced (as in "Frog Legs Rag" and "Honey Moon Rag") by unaccompanied bass octaves. Other Scott rags that suggest the opening measures of the "Maple Leaf" include "The Fascinator," "The Ragtime 'Betty,'" "Par-amount Rag," and "Troubadour Rag."

Interestingly, Scott never attempted to use the unusual harmonic structure of the first strain to "Maple Leaf," which included a modulation to the tonic minor and a dramatic return to the tonic via a diminished seventh chord. Perhaps he felt it was too closely identified with Joplin (who had used it in a number of other rags, most notably "Gladiolus," "Sugar Cane," and "The Cascades"). But it is also possible that its asymmetry and its bizarre harmonic twists simply held no appeal for him.

In general, Scott did not follow the example set by Joplin in devising novel and varied harmonic structures. Most of the strains stay narrowly within the boundaries of tonic and dominant. Still others move via a succession of secondary dominants through the circle of fifths, as in the D strain of "Ragtime Oriole" and the C strains of "Kansas City Rag," "Sunburst Rag," and "Pegasus." What is particularly striking are the harmonies *not* used. Joplin knew how to soften the relentless dominant tendencies of ragtime by deflecting the harmony to the subdominant side of the circle of fifths. (Joplin, for example, was fond of starting a strain in the subdominant, as in the B strains of "Palm Leaf Rag," "Wall Street Rag," or "Paragon Rag.") By contrast, Scott rarely used the subdominant, except as part of the typical drive toward the final cadence (e.g., in the progression IV–♯IV°–I⁶₄). "Troubadour Rag," with its occasional turns to the subdominant (B:11–12; C:1–4), is an exception that proves the rule. The dominant orientation of most of Scott's music lends it a certain brittleness and nervous energy that is only partially counterbalanced by the richness of the harmonic setting.

One contrasting harmony that Scott did use to great effectiveness was the mediant (iii). The mediant is often the harmonic goal of the first eight-bar period (or, more rarely, the strain itself). It is far enough removed from the tonic on the circle of fifths to provide a welcome sense of harmonic distance. But because the triad of the mediant is closely related to the tonic triad, the return to the home key is easy, almost casual. A good example is the end of the A strain of "Hilarity Rag" (mm. 13–16), where the A♭ tonality is interrupted by a strong cadence in C minor. Only one note in the C-minor chord—G—need be changed to return to A♭. And this is precisely what allows the C-minor tonality in the second ending of the A strain of "Hilarity Rag" to blend imperceptibly back into the home key at the beginning of the B strain.

Scott probably derived the idea of a temporary modulation to the mediant from Joplin, since it appears first in the passage from "A Summer Breeze" that is directly borrowed from Joplin's "Elite Syncopations." He quickly made this clever harmonic twist his own. It occurs in nearly half of the rags, often in several different strains, and in many different guises. In one particularly effective variant, he modulates more distantly to the parallel major of the mediant (e.g., from A♭ to C *major,* as in the final strain of "Rag Sentimental"). It is an effect as lovely and unforced as a ray of sunshine.

FORM

.

The larger-scale forms of all Scott's ragtime pieces are variations on the basic episodic, multistrain pattern used by every ragtime composer. Nearly all his rags begin with a four-bar introduction (those that do not do so in obvious homage to the "Maple Leaf"). Except for the early rags, these introductions are related thematically to the strain that immediately follows: anticipating its opening measures or (as in "Efficiency Rag" and "Ragtime Oriole") a particularly striking "measure 13" phrase.

The first half of all the rags comprises two strains, each with a full repetition. Most continue with a reprise of the A strain, creating the form AABBA, but a few (e.g., "Hilarity Rag") do not. The second half of the rag is set off by a modulation, almost always to the subdominant (or, in the case of rags in the minor mode, the subdominant of the relative major), marking the arrival of the trio, or third strain. In one-third of Scott's rags, the trio is preceded by a four-bar transition, the sole purpose of which is to transform the tonic into the dominant seventh of the new key.

The trio is sometimes followed by a fourth, or D, strain—a practice largely abandoned after 1911 (the exceptions are "Paramount Rag" and the leisurely "Rag Sentimental" and "Troubadour Rag"). More often, Scott concludes by bringing back the B strain, occasionally transposed to match the key of the trio. If the B strain returns in its original key, the modulation from the subdominant back to the tonic will often be effected by a four-bar transition as well. These internal transitions are generally unrelated to the rest of the piece and in some cases strongly suggest clichés from the concert march (see, for example, the nearly identical transitions in "Kansas City Rag" and "Prosperity Rag").

In most cases a strain is repeated verbatim if reprised. In a few of the later rags, Scott varied this practice by rewriting the concluding bars of a strain on its second appearance. The earliest example is the A strain of "Climax Rag" (1914); but the most elegant instance is the 1920 rag "Modesty," in which both the A and B strains are provided with luxuriant new endings.

The waltzes also follow an episodic, multistrain format, with a few significant adjustments: individual strains tend to be thirty-two, rather than sixteen, bars long, and the A strain tends to return, rondolike, for a third appearance at the end of the composition. As in the rags the C strain, or trio, is set off by a modulation to the subdominant, usually preceded by a short interlude establishing the dominant of the new key. The songs use the bipartite structure common to popular songs of the period, with a verse of indeterminate length leading into the chorus, a sixteen- or thirty-two-bar closed tonal form.

MELODIC MATERIALS

If by "melody" one means clearly defined cantabile phrases, Scott's music, like much of ragtime, is only rarely melodic. Single-note lines, even of the intricate, convoluted type favored by Joplin and Lamb, are more the exception than the rule. Instead, the basic melodic unit is a compact one- to two-measure pattern in which rhythm and melodic contour are fused into one memorable motive. A good example is the ascending three-note figure at the beginning of the second strain of "Grace and Beauty" (reused by Scott in the C strain of "Ophelia Rag" and the B strain of "Prosperity Rag").

Short melodic motives are often used as building blocks, to be preserved and extended through sequence (i.e., repetition at a different pitch level). In the opening strains of "Evergreen Rag," "Modesty Rag," and "Rag Sentimental," two-measure fragments are repeated sequentially at the distance of a fourth or fifth. More characteristically, repetition occurs at the octave: in Scott's trademark antiphonal leaps (e.g., "Great Scott Rag," B:3–8) or, as in the opening measures of "Quality" and "Ragtime Oriole," in a continuous melodic sweep. More often than not, however, it is the rhythmic, rather than the melodic, content of the motive that predominates—a symptom of the persistent use of one-measure rhythmic patterns so characteristic of Scott's music as a whole. A passage like the trio of "Evergreen Rag" is characterized more by the insistent use of a single rhythmic motive than by any melodic material.

At times chromatic passing and neighbor tones can make Scott's melodic lines quite complex. (The final strain of "Troubadour Rag" is a particularly fine example.) But in general the melodic lines are diatonic, even in more complicated passages, as if to counterbalance the intricate chromatic movement of the inner voices (note, for example, the introduction to "Efficiency Rag"). The overall impression is one of simplicity, even naïveté, heightened in certain passages by the use of the pentatonic scale. The openings of "Grace and Beauty" and its close cousin "Prosperity Rag" are the most obvious examples of pentatonic material. But even more conventional passages, such as the opening measures of "Sunburst Rag" and

"Ophelia Rag," are essentially pentatonic melodies enriched with neighbor motions.

Because many tunes from folk traditions are also pentatonic, Ann Charters has cited such passages as evidence for the influence of black folk music on ragtime. [10] The relationship between ragtime—and Scott's music in particular—and the black folk tradition is an interesting area for speculation, but one that should be approached with caution, if only because our knowledge of folk music of the time is sketchy and because the boundary between "folk" and other forms of vernacular music is not easy to draw. Pentatonicism is prevalent in Anglo-American as well as African American folk music, and it was well diffused into popular and salon music of the nineteenth century, including the music of Stephen Foster and the popular pseudoethnic "black character" piano pieces from the early days of ragtime. As a black man growing up in Missouri, as an American absorbed in popular music, and as a pianist in a music shop demonstrating the latest sheet music for customers, Scott would likely have been influenced by a variety of sources, any of which could have given him a taste for pentatonic melodies.

A more complicated issue involves the use in ragtime of "blue notes." [11] "Blue notes" may be briefly defined as an expressive ambivalence of pitch used in the blues and other forms of African American vocal music, usually focusing on the third and seventh degrees of the scale. Real pitch variability cannot, obviously, be reproduced on a fixed-pitch instrument like the piano. One way of approximating the effect is a dissonant cluster with a minor second at its core. This device is common in recordings by James P. Johnson and Jelly Roll Morton from the 1920s but appears only once in Scott's music, in a cadential passage in the 1920 "Pegasus" (C:16, second ending).

A simpler and less harsh way of suggesting pitch ambiguity is the embellishment of a given scale degree with its lower chromatic neighbor. This practice is used in the earliest published blues (see ex. 11) and is quite widespread in ragtime. Examples from Scott's own work include his first and last published rags: the 1903 "Fascinator" (e″–d♯″–e″, A:1) and the 1922 "Broadway Rag" (a♯–b, A:3). The extent to which such passages are intended to convey a bluesy sense of pitch ambiguity, on the other hand, is an open question. Certainly the "break" in the opening strain of "Kansas

10. Ann R. Danberg Charters, "Negro Folk Elements in Classic Ragtime," *Ethnomusicology* 5 (1961): 174–83.

11. Ibid., 177; Addison Walker Reed, "The Life and Works of Scott Joplin" (Ph.D. diss., University of North Carolina, 1973), 127.

City Rag" (A:13–14) seems like a blues gesture, however stylized. But the more immediate function of such passages is *rhythmic*. Neighbor motions tend to form discrete two- or three-note motives that clearly define the additive groupings essential to ragtime polyrhythm (see ex. 12).

Example 11. A. Maggio, "I Got the Blues" (1908), A:2–6 (left-hand part)

Example 12. James Scott, "Sunburst Rag," A:7–8 (left-hand part)

However much significance one wishes to attach to the use of "blue notes" or pentatonic passages in Scott's writing, the primary evidence for the influence of the black folk tradition lies elsewhere. One of the defining features of his style, for example, is the use of call-and-response patterns, with melodic material thrown back and forth between different registers in the right hand. The similarity between these call-and-response patterns and practices in black musical traditions such as the spiritual and the work song is obvious (although Scott seems as likely to have absorbed the device from other pianists as from these vocal genres). Above all, there is the percussive, multilayered rhythmic texture that pervades every measure. Even in the absence of any other evidence, the use of rhythm alone would securely mark Scott's music as African American in origin.

PIANO TEXTURE

The composers of ragtime were by and large highly skilled professional pianists, an elite fraternity of which James Scott was a member. One contemporary who remembered Scott from his tenure at the Lincoln Theatre in Kansas City in the 1920s admiringly described him as the "number one" pianist in the city, a man who had "execution."[12] What distinguishes Scott in retrospect from his peers is not so much his technical ability—it is impossible, in any case, to judge at this historical distance how Scott would have compared with such legendary virtuosos as James P. Johnson or fellow Missourian Tom Turpin—as the extent to which he poured his

12. Marvin Van-Gilder, "James Scott," in *Ragtime: Its History, Composers, and Music*, ed. John Edward Hasse (New York: Schirmer Books, 1985), 143.

energy into richly detailed and accurately notated compositions. Through these pieces we can come to know Scott the pianist.

Scott's music requires considerable technique—certainly more than was normally expected from the amateur pianists who bought the sheet music. In the final strain of the early "A Summer Breeze," the performer is given the option (presumably by the publisher, Dumars) of replacing the octaves in the score with single notes. It is a tribute to John Stark that no such concessions are to be found in the music published by his firm. Indeed, many of the rags leave a dauntingly dense visual impression (especially in the later pieces when, for economy's sake, Stark reduced an entire composition to two pages).

Still, the pieces are generally less difficult than they might at first glance appear. Scott's writing is consistently idiomatic, reflecting his working knowledge of what would be practical at the keyboard. Much of the motivic material consists of patterns that fall easily within the compass of the hand: alternations of single notes and chords, for example, as in the trio of "Pegasus," or the broken octaves of "Hilarity Rag" (A strain) and "Rag Sentimental" (B strain). Linking one such set of patterns with another, however, often requires rapid shifts of hand position—especially with call-and-response patterns, where leaps back and forth of an octave are common. Among the trickiest of these passages occurs near the beginning of "Modesty Rag," where the shift must be effected within a continuous, legato sixteenth-note melodic line (A:5–6).

For all its technical sophistication, Scott's music is rarely flashy; it does not depend on the pianistic "tricks" that all professionals cultivated (and that Artie Matthews displayed so whimsically in his own "Pastime Rags"). The greatest technical challenge arises from the way in which the composer conceived his thematic material. Typically, Scott scored a melody not as a single-note line but in octaves. These octaves, moreover, tend to be filled in by densely voiced harmonies—recalling the observation by Scott's cousin that "he liked playing as many notes as possible under one beat with the right hand."[13]

In much piano music such a thick texture would be reserved for a particularly powerful or climactic passage. With Scott it is the norm. Given its prevailingly cheerful and optimistic mood and elegantly worked-out harmonies, the music must be played lightly and crisply, without pounding. In passages such as the B strain of "Hilarity Rag" or the trio of

---

13. Rudi Blesh and Harriet Janis, *They All Played Ragtime* (New York: Oak Publications, 1971), 115.

"Efficiency Rag," the challenge for the performer is not simply to play all the notes (as difficult as that may be) but to convey the essential simplicity of the melodic style in a relaxed as well as precise manner. The difficulty of the task is compounded by the fact that the rags tend to be highly concentrated pieces requiring intense bursts of energy, with few, if any, resting places. It is here that Scott's pianistic gifts—consisting of endurance as well as power and accuracy—can best be appreciated.

The great joy in Scott's music comes from the variety of pianistic textures. No other ragtime composer took such obvious delight in exploiting the full range of the piano keyboard—or of breaking down the stereotypical division of labor between the pianist's left and right hands. There are a number of passages in which the left hand unexpectedly breaks away from the "boom-chick" foundation pattern: moving rapidly in octaves or arpeggios (e.g., "New Era Rag," C:4–5), leaping into the middle and upper registers to add a connecting inner voice (e.g., "Efficiency Rag," B:7–8), or simply taking over the melodic role from the right hand (e.g., "Rag Sentimental," B:3–5). Such inventiveness, exhilarating in itself, gives Scott's oeuvre much of its aesthetic range. The more athletic side of ragtime is represented by vigorous, extroverted pieces like "Efficiency Rag" and "Peace and Plenty Rag." But the beautiful "Modesty Rag," on the other hand, is a piece of extraordinary delicacy, requiring a singing touch and a subtle weighting of melody and inner voices; it has few parallels in the entire ragtime repertory.

PERFORMANCE PRACTICE

For the users of this edition, how to interpret the notes on the printed page will be a matter of practical concern. For the historian the issue of performance practice poses several knotty problems that remain to be resolved satisfactorily. There is, first of all, the question of improvisation. The performing tradition out of which ragtime arose relied heavily on the ability of pianists to "fake" (i.e., improvise) and "rag" existing pieces through complicated rhythmic (and possibly harmonic) elaboration. Composed ragtime is thus but one aspect of a broader sphere of musical activity, and many surviving ragtime scores are patently sketchy and incomplete— blueprints for a more detailed and spontaneous realization by the performer.

In light of this it might seem inappropriate to insist on a fastidiously literal rendering of these, or any other, ragtime scores. And yet ragtime performance practice formed a wide spectrum. Just as there were musicians who played entirely by ear, there were those who preferred to work out their music entirely in written form. Scott, along with Joplin (who in his *School of Ragtime* explained that his music was "harmonized with the supposition that each note will be played as it is written"), would appear to be among the latter.

This is not to say that a modest amount of improvisation—or perhaps more accurately, variation—is never allowable or appropriate. In a number of instances Scott provides different figuration for the same passage—enough to suggest that some liberty may be taken with inventing new patterns, especially bass lines, when material is repeated. As with any ragtime this must be done with care and is best left to those with both the imagination and sensitivity to stylistic nuance to do the job tastefully. (The skilled jazz improviser is of course free to use any rag, including Scott's, as the framework for further elaboration.) In any case, with Scott's music there is no *need* to improvise. The pieces as they stand are completely self-sufficient and need no further elaboration. Many performers will undoubtedly prefer to approach this music as one would approach the European classical repertoire: with the notes and rhythms to be studied and learned as they appear on the page.

That having been said, even a literal rendering of Scott's music leaves a great deal of creative responsibility in the hands of the performer. Indications for dynamics, phrasing, articulation, and other important performance details appear only sporadically; where they do exist, they are generally ambiguous, incomplete, inconsistent, or otherwise difficult to interpret. A more detailed discussion of these problems may be found in the essay on editorial policy that follows. For the moment, two points should be made. First, the passages in which such markings appear with some consistency (e.g., the first two strains of "Grace and Beauty") make it clear that Scott's conception of his music involved a good deal of expressive shading—not the sort of monochromatic reading familiar from machine-cut piano rolls. In his expressive gestures, as in his harmonic language, Scott was a child of late nineteenth-century musical romanticism (the twentieth-century percussiveness of the rhythm notwithstanding). Second, the absence of such markings should be taken not as a proscription against expressiveness but as a vacuum to be filled by the performer. Armed with these ideas, each individual ought to be able to find his or her own way to an aesthetically satisfying realization of Scott's music.

The rhythmic dimension presents a different set of problems. Scott was a pianist in the African American tradition, and his ragtime pieces ought to have the rhythmically propulsive quality of "swing." Lacking this quality, in fact, they will lose not only much of their charm but also their distinctiveness. Swing is a notoriously difficult concept to define or describe, much less to produce. But it may help to say that in any music that swings the articulation, while precise, should be supple and legato rather than brittle. Above all, the different polyrhythmic layers—the additive patterns in the right hand "dancing" above the steady rhythmic foundation of the left hand—must be clearly projected.

Whether or not to use the "swing eighth notes" of more modern African American piano playing, in which the notated rhythm is treated as an unequal division of the beat, is another question. Contemporary machine-cut piano rolls of Scott's music invariably play the eighth notes as written, and as the work of many modern ragtime pianists shows, a swinging effect can be achieved in this way. But rhythmic sensibility was in a state of continuous evolution during Scott's lifetime. By the beginning of the 1920s, evidence for a looser rhythmic feeling can be heard in recordings by Jelly Roll Morton and James P. Johnson, and even (albeit to a lesser degree) in such recordings as Fred Van Eps's and Frank Banta's piano-banjo version of "Ragtime Oriole" from 1923.[14] There is also an intriguing bit of evidence in the notation at the beginning of "Troubadour Rag" (1919), where equal sixteenth notes alternate with the unequal combination of a dotted sixteenth and thirty-second (played as written by William Bolcom in his 1974 recording).[15] Perhaps Scott in his later years was adapting to a new and more modern rhythmic style (he was, after all, a contemporary of Count Basie in Kansas City). In any case, the historical record is ambiguous enough to support a variety of interpretations, and the performer may choose whatever style seems appropriate for the music.

More than a century has now passed since James Scott's birth. In the intervening years a whole musical style came to life, passed into obscurity, and was rescued by the vigorous efforts of enthusiasts and scholars. The "ragtime revival" has returned this music to the American mainstream, where it currently receives a respect and critical attention that was only grudgingly, if ever, accorded it on its initial appearance. It no longer seems strange to refer to a black theater pianist from Missouri as an important American composer. The evidence, in any case, is in the music, presented here for the first time as a complete repertory. The sheet music covers, the

---

14. Recorded as "The Oriole" on 28 September 1923 (Pathé Actuelle 021088).

15. *Pastimes & Piano Rags,* Nonesuch H-71299.

languid waltzes, and sentimental parlor songs may evoke in many a nostalgia for turn-of-the-century America, a period distant to modern sensibilities. But within the ragtime compositions is an artistic tension—a "grace and beauty"—that is shared by the best pieces in the African American tradition and that is the quality found in all lasting art. It is altogether fitting that this music be placed back in the hands of the American public, for whom it was originally written.

EDITORIAL POLICY

SOURCES ONLY ONE SOURCE EXISTS for each of the compositions by James Scott—the published version, reproduced here in facsimile. Two pieces, "Dixie Dimples" and "Springtime of Love," were each published in successive years by the Will L. Livernash Company (Kansas City) and Seidel Music Publishing Company (Indianapolis), respectively. Aside from publisher's imprint and date of copyright (1919 instead of 1918 for the two Seidel prints), the Livernash and Seidel editions appear to have been identical. The present edition reproduces the 1919 (Seidel) edition of "Springtime of Love," since no copy of the 1918 (Livernash) print has been found.

The editors have chosen to include in this edition only those pieces published during Scott's lifetime that can unambiguously be attributed to him. One widely circulated piece that fails to meet these criteria is "Calliope Rag." The origins of this rag are obscure. One of Scott's sisters is said to have given a partial, damaged manuscript to Robert ("Ragtime Bob") Darch, who, along with ragtime performer Donald Ashwander, "arranged and edited" it for publication in the 1966 edition of Blesh's and Janis's *They All Played Ragtime.* Since the original manuscript has never surfaced, it is impossible to know exactly what was "arranged and edited," or to form an opinion on the rag's authenticity. On stylistic grounds there is little evidence to link this piece to James Scott. The harmonic language is simple, the pianistic texture (by Scott's standards) unimaginative. (Of course, Scott may well have adjusted his style to a new performing medium—the calliope.) Certain features—especially the truncated eight-measure trio, but also the use of sixteenth-note triplets in the B and C strains and the unusual procedure in the B strain of repeating measures 1–7 an octave higher—have no precedent in Scott's oeuvre. Because doubts remain about its authenticity, "Calliope Rag" has not been included in this edition. References to recordings and scores of this piece can be found in the appendixes to the edition.

Another problematic case is the song "I Feel Like Sending Home for Money," published by the W. C. Polla Company in Chicago in 1905. The composer is listed on the first page of the music as James Scott, but on the cover the name is given as "J. W. Scott." The middle initial is enough to cast serious doubt on the relationship of this song to James Sylvester Scott; other considerations only deepen that doubt. It seems unlikely that Scott, still a teenager in a small Missouri town, would have come to the attention of a Chicago publisher, and have been asked (presumably by mail) to collaborate with lyricist Irving Jones; or that the fledgling composer would have been allowed to dedicate the song prominently "to my Sincere Friend Edna Esmeralda" (a name that we have been unable to link to Neosho or Carthage). It is even more unlikely that Scott would have consented to work on a song of this nature. "I Feel Like Sending Home for Money" is the story of a "coon" named Sam Jones who wins a thousand dollars in a crap game, only to rapidly squander his fortune. After losing three hundred dollars in one game, "he look'd so pale you'd thought that he was white." While the music to the song and Scott's early rags have a generic similarity (the chorus of the song and the C strain of "On the Pike" have the cakewalk rhythm and circle-of-fifths harmonic movement in common), the song is much clumsier in its voice leading and contains uncharacteristically static harmonic passages. For these reasons, "I Feel Like Sending Home for Money" has not been included in this edition.

CRITERIA FOR
EMENDATION

In one respect, the lack of manuscripts or other source material simplifies editorial procedure: there is no need to sort through the evidence to establish priority among competing versions. At the same time, the original scores abound in typographical errors, editorial oversights, and notational inconsistencies. Such corruptions of the text need to be corrected, for the sake of the performer as well as for the integrity of the music. In *The Music of James Scott,* we have tried to strike a balance between the requirements of a facsimile and a modern edition, intervening to correct substantive mistakes, while preserving as much as possible the appearance and content of the original publication as a historical document.

Most of the editorial changes concern obvious errors. To avoid cluttering the page, we have not identified editorial emendations (additions, deletions, and alterations) on the music itself. All such changes, however, are reported in the Critical Commentary section of this book. The Critical Commentary also discusses in detail some of the difficult problems of interpreting text, dynamics, and articulation in certain passages. The present essay outlines the broader editorial philosophy underlying emendations of the original text.

The notation used in the original published version, however awkward, unorthodox, or confusing by modern standards, has generally been retained, as long as it does not obscure unduly the sense of the original text. Thus, irregular clusterings of notes around the stem, incorrect stem directions, and unorthodox spelling of chromatic notes have not been altered. Adjustments have been made only where, in our judgment, the original notation makes it unnecessarily difficult for the performer to interpret the text. One example of a passage that has been changed is measure B:12 of "Grace and Beauty" ("B" refers to the second or B strain, "12" to the measure number within the strain—see "The Music of James Scott," above, and the section "Terminology," below). The original rhythmic notation in the right hand can be notated more simply and legibly as it is in this edition (see ex. 13). Other violations of convention that have been emended include the presence of rests in the bass clef when the left-hand part moves into the treble clef (the absence of rests in the bass clef is designed to make it clear at a glance that the lower voice is not "resting" but is currently active in another clef); inaccurate cues for clef changes; and, in vocal settings, the absence of extender lines to indicate that a syllable is to be sung through more than one pitch.

Example 13. James Scott, "Grace and Beauty," B:12, right hand, original and edited versions

For the most part two main criteria have governed corrections in this edition: common sense and internal consistency. "Common sense" here is based upon a knowledge of the idiom—or, more precisely, sensitivity to notated passages patently out of place within the idiom, as with the many typographical errors that result in gross dissonance. For example, at the end of the four-measure interlude (abbreviated "Int") preceding the trio (or C strain) in "Frog Legs Rag," a sharply accented minor seventh (F–e♭)

occurs. No performer would ever have played this interval where an octave is clearly intended. The error is presumably typographical. Notes placed a line or space too high or low on the staff, omitted ledger lines, and missing ties—such mistakes occur with some frequency in the original published text. Correcting obvious errors is a main priority in this edition.

A different, less dramatic, category of error results from a lack of care in notation. Repeat bars, for example, are absent from the beginning of many strains. A performer reading the original published version of "Sunburst Rag" might not even notice that the first strain lacks a double bar to mark its beginning. The repeat sign at the end of the first strain would seem to require a return to the very beginning of the piece, that is, to the introduction (Intro). Those familiar with the conventions of ragtime will know that a return to the beginning of the strain, and not to the introduction, is intended. To remove any ambiguity, all such missing repeat signs have been added in this edition. (Strains that are not repeated are usually set off by thin-thin double barlines at the beginning and end, to clarify the division of the piece into its formal units. Where such double bars are lacking, they have been added in this edition.)

Perhaps the most frequent errors involve carelessly omitted or misplaced accidentals. Again, the context is often so clear that the error might not even be noticed. In the original published version of "Sunburst Rag," no accidental appears in front of the last octave in the left hand of A2:12. At first glance none would seem to be needed. But technically, the d♭ earlier in the measure is still in effect. To preserve musical sense a natural sign is required in front of the d.

In the Trio of the same piece, the accidental that appears in front of f″ in the right hand in the fourth measure (C:4) ought to be a sharp (as in the edition) rather than a natural (as in the original). Making this correction produces a second problem: a now superfluous sharp on f″ in the next chord. That accidental has been deleted here, and the same procedure has been followed for all other redundant accidentals. Where, however, an accidental, even if not literally needed, serves as a useful reminder to the performer that another accidental in the previous measure is no longer in effect, it has been retained. A good example is the natural before g″ on the downbeat of the same strain's second measure (C:2). While not absolutely required, it warns the performer not to carry over the sharp on g″ from the preceding measure. Such "cautionary" accidentals have been retained from the original published text and by extension have been added, where useful, to similar measures that may have lacked them in the original. Otherwise, editorial cautionaries have not been newly added.

The second main criterion for determining error is internal consistency. Ragtime is a highly symmetric music, with repetition occurring at many different levels. Entire sixteen-bar strains are, of course, repeated. In addition, because of the symmetric phrase construction, material may well appear several times within a sixteen-bar strain. If a particular passage is heard in the first measure, it is likely to be heard again in measure 9, and possibly measures 5 and 13 as well. Certain passages—especially cadential material—may well be shared by several different strains, and perhaps also by the introduction.

Ragtime's pervasive repetition helps to identify typographical errors. Comparing one otherwise identical passage with another is a particularly valuable means of determining a correct reading. "Hilarity Rag" provides a typical example. Toward the end of the final strain (D:15), the chords in the left hand form an inexplicable dissonant cluster (see ex. 14). Because the same passage occurs at the end of the preceding strain (C:15), it is clear that the cluster resulted from placing the lower two notes of the chord a step too high. Internal consistency also provides an excellent check on decisions arrived at by the "common sense" method. That the natural sign on the downbeat of C:4 in "Sunburst Rag" should be replaced by a sharp, as discussed earlier, is easily confirmed by comparing C:4 with the otherwise identical measure in the second half of the strain, C:12, where the sharp appears.

Example 14. James Scott, "Hilarity Rag," D:15, left hand, original version

Wherever different versions of the same passage are equally plausible from a musical point of view, decisions are less easy to reach. In some instances the quantitative weight of evidence can be used to favor one reading over another. As a case in point, throughout the B strain of "Quality," the Eb dominant chord in the left hand is voiced sometimes as a three-note chord (eb–g–db′) and sometimes a four-note chord (eb–g–bb–db′). While there is no obvious musical reason to prefer one chord to the other, the four-note version appears only twice (B1:2, 9), in comparison with seven appearances of the three-note chord. When the whole strain is repeated at the end of the rag, only the three-note chord is used. Evidence suggests, therefore, that the fourth note in the chord is a typographical error, and it has been deleted in this edition.

It may be argued that a procedure like this one imposes an artificial uniformity on the music, eliminating variations within similar material that the composer may have intended. In this edition, where internal discrepancies carry legitimate musical significance, the policy has been to retain them. This happens very rarely: the slight change in the octave melody in the trio of "Efficiency Rag" (C:1–2, 5–6) might be considered one example. In the example cited above from "Quality," as in many other pieces, the variant seems too insignificant to be intentional. This is admittedly a matter of judgment; wherever the original text has been changed, a full explanation of the change and the reasoning behind it appears in the Critical Commentary, under "Comments."

Quite often there are no firm grounds for choosing between two competing readings. In "Evergreen Rag" the two appearances of the B strain diverge in a number of minor details of pitch and rhythm. Each version is equally plausible: whether, for example, to give the left-hand octave in measure 8 the rhythmic value of a quarter note, as in B1, or an eighth note, as in B2. In such cases the discrepancies have been duly noted, but no changes have been made.

While Scott (or his publisher) exercised considerable care in the notation of pitch and rhythm in his pieces, performance marks were treated far more haphazardly. Indications for dynamics, articulation, tempo, and expression appear only sporadically. Where they do appear, they are often ambiguous and internally inconsistent. Such performance markings pose problems of interpretation for the editor—problems not always easy to resolve.

Dynamic Marks

Dynamic marks in Scott's music fall into two categories:

1. Markings at the beginning of a strain. These general indications are meant to cover the entire strain. For strains that are repeated, there is frequently a double marking (e.g., *mf–f*) specifying a different dynamic level for each appearance.
2. Crescendo and decrescendo indications within a strain, generally for expressive purposes. These usually take the form of hairpin markings.

Many strains are modified by only the single dynamic marking in their opening measure. Most, however, carry at least some explicit indication for expressive variation in volume. Crescendos and decrescendos tend to follow the rise and fall of the melodic line, highlighting the phrase structure measure by measure. Passages in which expressive dynamic markings are most carefully laid out—the A strain of "Grace and Beauty" or the B strain of "Don't Jazz Me—Rag," for example—fit Scott's harmonic and melodic language so naturally that they argue persuasively for the similar expressive use of dynamics even where not explicitly indicated (but this is a matter of speculation).

Problems of interpreting dynamics in Scott's music arise primarily from the inconsistent use of markings. Typical problems include (1) strains without dynamic markings, (2) discrepancies in dynamic markings between two otherwise identical versions of a strain, (3) discrepancies in the use of dynamic markings within a strain, and (4) illogical sequences of dynamic markings.

In general, dynamic markings seem to be underrepresented in Scott's music. Their omission appears to have been a matter of carelessness or expediency on the part of either the composer or the publisher (or both). Typically, markings are given for a passage on its first appearance and are dropped thereafter. While it may seem reasonable to assume that the same manner of performance is intended for subsequent passages, the situation is not always so clear-cut. In "Rag Sentimental," for example, detailed dynamic markings appear in A2 but not in A1.

Ambiguities of this sort are more the rule than the exception, making it impossible to determine Scott's "usual" procedure. Such is the case with strains that lack dynamic markings. Of the twenty-two of Scott's rags that open with the structure A1–B–A2, ten lack a marking for A2. In most such cases, A1 has a marking of *mf*, B a marking of *f* (see table 2). Should A2 continue at the increased volume level of the intervening B strain? Such is the case in "Frog Legs Rag," "Climax Rag," and "Prosperity Rag." But in six other pieces the dynamic level of A2 is identical with A1. This practice, which reinforces the symmetry of the ternary ABA structure, is predominant in Scott Joplin's rags, with *mf*–*f*–*mf* by far the most common pattern (see table 3). Was A1 = A2 a performance convention, to be followed when A2 lacked a dynamic marking? This is an attractive hypothesis, but in the absence of more concrete evidence, no firm conclusion can be reached.

In this edition few additions or changes have been made to the dynamic markings that appear in the original published text. Ambiguities of the sort discussed above are addressed in the Critical Commentary, under "Comments."

Articulation Marks   Articulation marks of several kinds—slurs, staccato marks, accent marks—are found throughout Scott's music. Staccato and accent marks present few editorial problems, except when they are applied inconsistently in otherwise identical material. (In such cases the original published text has generally been retained, with discrepancies noted in the Critical Commentary.) Slurs, on the other hand, are much more difficult. They tend to be applied with little regard for consistency. Even under the best of circumstances, it is unclear precisely what information they are intended to convey.

TABLE 2. *Dynamic Markings in Scott's Rags*

TITLE	A1	B	A2
A2 lacking			
The Fascinator	*mf*	*f*	—
On the Pike	*mf*	*f*	—
Grace and Beauty	*mf*	*f*	—
The Ragtime "Betty"	*mf*	*f*	—
Quality	*mf–p*	*mf–f*	—
Ragtime Oriole	*mf*	*f*	—
Efficiency Rag	*f*	*mf*	—
Peace and Plenty Rag	*mf*	*f*	—
Troubadour Rag	*mf*	*f*	—
Broadway Rag	*mf*	*f*	—
A1 = A2			
A Summer Breeze	*mf*	*mf*	*mf*
Sunburst Rag	*f*	*p–mf*	*f*
Honey Moon Rag	*f*	*ff*	*f*
Dixie Dimples	*mf*	*mf*	*mf*
Rag Sentimental	*mf*	*mp–f*	*mf*
Modesty Rag	*mf*	*mf*	*mf*
A1 ≠ A2			
Frog Legs Rag	*mf*	*f*	*f*
Climax Rag	*mf*	*f*	*f*
Prosperity Rag	*mf*	*f*	*f*
Don't Jazz Me—Rag	*mf*	*mp–mf*	*f*
A1 lacking			
Victory Rag	—	*f*	*mf*
A1, A2 lacking			
New Era Rag (Intro: *f*)	—	—	—

A few slurs may be attributed to idiosyncratic habits of notation. It was an occasional practice, for example, for Scott to slur groups of sixteenth notes immediately preceding the first measure of a strain. Such slurs are often isolated (rarely continuing to the following downbeat) and seem to have little to do with articulation (see, for example, "Modesty Rag," Intro:4, A:8, A:16a; "Rag Sentimental," A2:16; "Sunburst Rag," A:16b, B:16a). Slurs also tend to be used more frequently in connecting passages—introductions and interludes—than elsewhere.

The most consistent and logical use of slurs in Scott's music is the isolation, by means of articulation, of a short, rhythmically distinct mo-

TABLE 3. *Dynamic Markings in Joplin's Rags*

TITLE	A1	B	A2
A2 lacking			
Cleopha	*f*	—	—
Strenuous Life	*f*	—	—
A1 = A2			
Maple Leaf	*f*	*f*	*f*
Entertainer	*p*	*f*	*p*
Weeping Willow	*f*	*f*	*f*
The Favorite	*mf*	*mf*	*mf*
Chrysanthemum	*mf*	*f*	*mf*
Leola	*mf*	*f*	*mf*
Eugenia	*mf*	*f*	*mf*
Gladiolus	*mf*	*f*	*mf*
Sugar Cane	*mf*	*f*	*mf*
Pine Apple	*mf*	*mf*	*mf*
Solace	*mf*	*f*	*mf*
Country Club	*mf*	*f*	*mf*
Euphonic Sounds	*mf*	*mf*	*mf*
Paragon	*mf*	*mp*	*mf*
Scott Joplin's New Rag	*mf*	*mp*	*mf*
Searchlight	*mf*	*f*	*mf*
Rose Leaf	*mf*	*mf*	*mf*
Fig Leaf	*mf*	*f*	*mf*
A1 ≠ A2: none			
A1, A2 lacking			
Peacherine	—	—	—
Easy Winners	—	—	—
Elite Syncopations	—	—	—

tive. Slurs over two-note motives are particularly common: the pairs of double sixteenth notes in the opening measures of the A strain of "Paramount Rag" (a common pianistic device in ragtime) are a good example. A related two-note grouping, beginning on a weak beat, may be seen in "Hilarity Rag" (B:13) and "Sunburst Rag" (Int:2–4). A different motive used with some frequency, especially in the later rags, is the figure shown in example 15. This motive, usually highlighted by slurs, is prominent in the A strain of "Quality," the B strains of "Honey Moon Rag," "Troubadour Rag," and "Efficiency Rag," and the C strains of "Peace and Plenty Rag," "Ophelia Rag," and "Victory Rag."

Example 15. Prominent motive often highlighted by slur

Where slurs outlining distinct motives have been omitted and, by context, are clearly intended, they have been reinstated in this edition. More often than not, however, an element of ambiguity precludes editorial intervention.

Discrepancies in the slurring of otherwise identical passages are common. Slurs may be of different lengths—extending to the following downbeat in some instances and falling short in others (e.g., "Victory Rag," B1:1–4 and B2:1–4). Slurs may be found over some appearances of a given motive and not over others. Where no evidence strongly supports one interpretation over the other, the slurring of the original text has been retained, with discrepancies noted in the Critical Commentary.

Aside from these relatively narrow categories, what do the slurs in Scott's music mean? They may, first of all, be taken as a general indication to play legato. In this sense the pervasiveness of slurring is a useful corrective to the common amateur tendency to perform ragtime with an overly percussive, detached touch. It should not be assumed, however, that only those passages under a slur should be played legato, and the remainder with a more detached articulation. The application of the slurs is too haphazard for so categorical an interpretation.

Nor are slurs of much practical help in delineating musical phrases. In a few instances slurs clearly outline long melodic phrases—enough to raise expectations that this may be the case elsewhere. Only rarely, however, do the slurs correspond with the phrases. Most slurs are short, rarely extending beyond the barline. In many cases a long, legato phrase is broken up by several different slurs, each one terminating at a barline or at a tied note. That this is a quirk of notation rather than a deliberate attempt to establish phrasing is evident from the many discrepancies between different appearances of identical material. To cite one of many examples, the descending bass line in the Trio of "New Era Rag" is placed under one slur in C:1–2 but is broken up by two slurs in C:9–10.

It is likely, in any case, that the actual phrases should be much longer. It makes little sense to break up the arching melodic line at the beginning of "Ragtime Oriole" (A:1–4) into measure-long fragments, for example. It makes even less sense for a long slur to stop just short of an obvious melodic goal, as in "Victory Rag," Int:1–3. To judge from these examples, as well as the many internal inconsistencies from passage to passage, and from strain to strain, little care seems to have been put into slur markings either by Scott or his publishers. Ultimately, decisions about articulation and phrasing must be left to the performer; and in many cases these decisions may contradict the existing markings. Lacking any clear criteria for superseding these markings with more coherent and consistent phrasing indications, however, the notation in the original published text has been left intact in this edition.

Vocal Texts For vocal texts and other verbal material in the scores (dedications, composer credits, and so on), the criteria for emending the original are the general standards of orthography. It may be of some slight historical interest, for example, to know that the composer was listed as "Jamas Scott" on the first page of "Sweetheart Time," or that the chorus of that song ended with the phrase "We will have to be good untill their in the mood / For its sweetheart time." But for the sake of coherence all such obvious misspellings have been corrected, with changes noted in the Critical Commentary. In addition, hyphens separating the syllables of a multisyllable word have been inserted wherever a space between the syllables indicates that the absence of a hyphen was unintentional. Other orthographic or grammatical peculiarities—punctuation, capitalization—have not been altered.

TITLES On a few occasions the title of a piece on the cover differs from the title as it appears on the music itself (the so-called caption title). For example, the cover to "On the Pike" reads "On the Pike—March-Two Step," whereas the full caption title is "On the Pike—(A Rag-time Two-Step)." The policy in this edition has been to assume the caption title to be authoritative, on the grounds that the title may well have been altered on the cover to fit an artistic design.

TERMINOLOGY The sixteen-bar (or thirty-two-bar) "strain" is the basic structural unit for all of Scott's rags and waltzes. Strains are identified in this edition by letters (placed in square brackets in the scores): the first strain is A, the second strain is B, the third strain (or "Trio") is C, and so forth. When a strain appears more than once, each of its appearances is indicated by a number following the letter: for example, A1 and A2 for the two appearances of the opening strain. Four-bar passages before the opening strain are called introductions, abbreviated as "Intro." Similar passages in the middle of the piece are called interludes, abbreviated as "Int." Where two interludes are found in a given piece, they are differentiated as "Int1" and "Int2." In the songs the structural units are a verse (of variable length) and a chorus (or refrain) of either sixteen or thirty-two bars.

Specific measures within a piece are identified by strain, with the numbering beginning anew for each strain. Thus, the first measure of the second strain would be identified as "B:1." Where a strain has separate first and second endings, measures in the first ending carry the suffix "a," while measures in the second ending carry the suffix "b" (e.g., A:15a, B:16b). All measure numbers in the edition are editorial and are added tacitly by 2s for each strain.

 THE WORKS OF JAMES SCOTT

 RAGS

A Summer Breeze.

March and Two Step.

JAMES SCOTT.

❋ If the octaves are too difficult play the lower notes.

THE FASCINATOR.

MARCH AND TWO-STEP.

JAMES SCOTT.

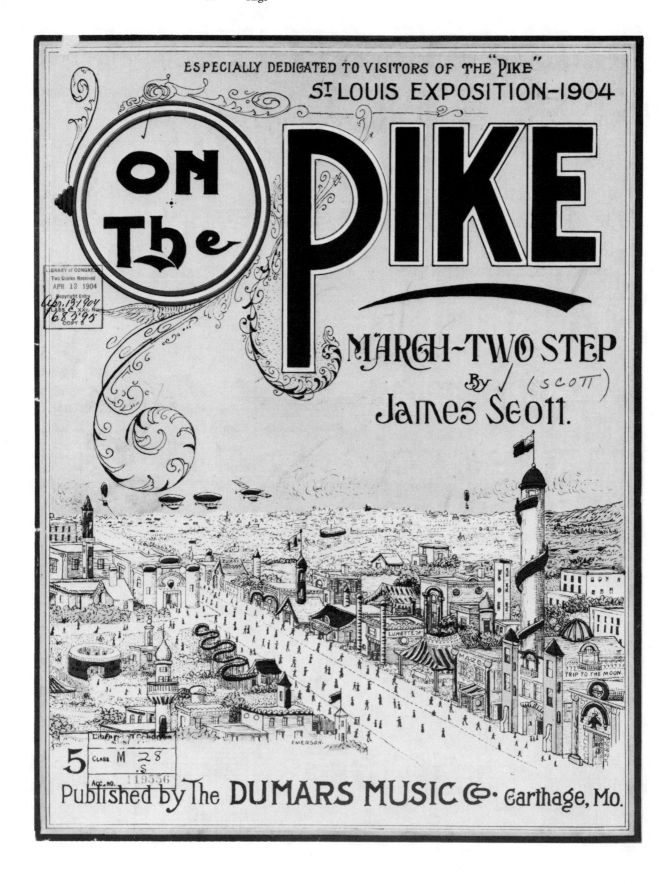

ON THE PIKE.

(A Rag-time Two-Step.)

JAMES SCOTT.

TRIO. *Repeat 8va.*

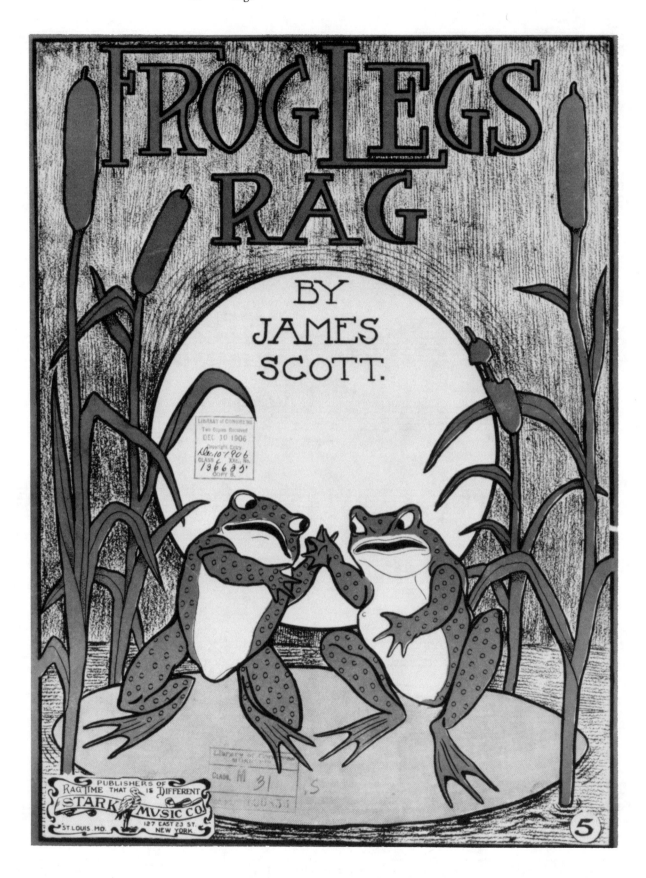

Frog Legs Rag.

JAMES SCOTT.

Kansas City Rag.

JAMES SCOTT.
Composer of " Frog Legs!"

Not too fast.

43-3

D.S. 𝄋 al Fine.

GRACE AND BEAUTY.

(a classy Rag.)

N.B. Do not play this piece fast,
Composer.

JAMES SCOTT.

By James Scott,
Composer of Frog Legs.
GREAT
SCOTT
RAG
COPYRIGHTED AND PUBLISHED
BY
ALLEN MUSIC CO.,
COLUMBIA MO.,

Great Scott Rag

JAMES SCOTT.
Comp. of "Frog Legs Rag."

The Ragtime "Betty."

By JAMES SCOTT.

SUNBURST RAG.

JAMES SCOTT.
Com. of *FROG LEGS RAG.*

Not fast.

© CLE240576
Music Division,
Reserve Storage.
HILARITY
RAG
PITCHERS
3 SHOTS
5 CENTS
BY JAMES SCOTT
5
STARK MUSIC CO.
3818 LACLEDE AVENUE.
ST. LOUIS, MO.

HILARITY RAG.

JAMES SCOTT.
Comp."Frog Legs."

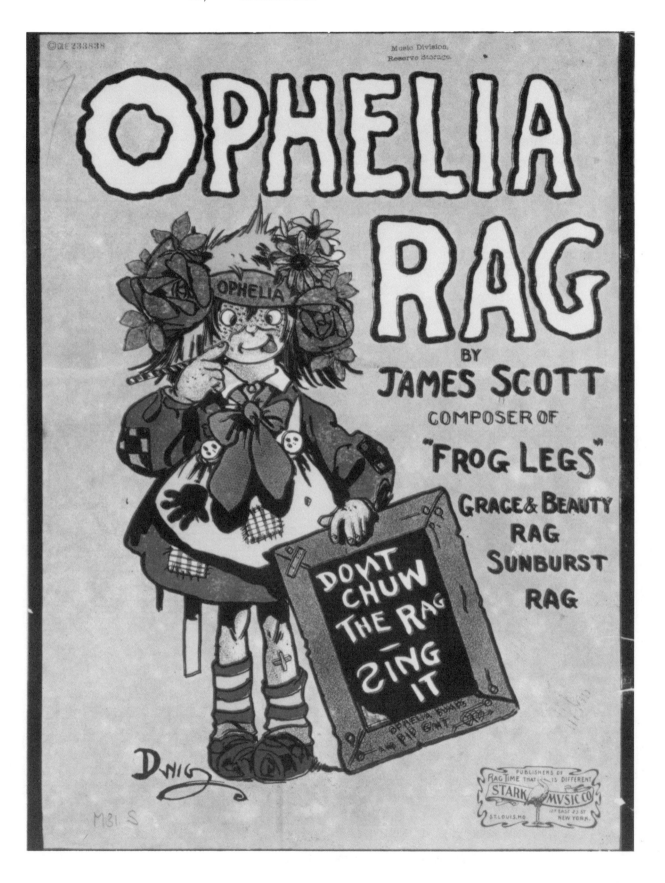

OPHELIA RAG.

JAMES SCOTT
Com. of "Frog Legs."

Not fast.

TRIO.

THE PRINCESS RAG.

JAMES SCOTT.

Comp. of Frog Legs Rag

Not too fast.

Quality
A HIGH CLASS RAG
BY
JAMES SCOTT
5
Publishers —
STARK MUSIC CO.
3818 Laclede ave. St. Louis.

QUALITY.

A HIGH CLASS RAG.

JAMES SCOTT.

RAGTIME ORIOLE.

James Scott.
Composer of Frog Legs Rag.

Do not play this piece fast.

Climax Rag.

JAMES SCOTT.

Evergreen Rag.

JAMES SCOTT.

Honey Moon Rag

JAMES SCOTT
Composer of Grace & Beauty

Do not play this piece fast.

Copyright 1916 by Stark Music Co.

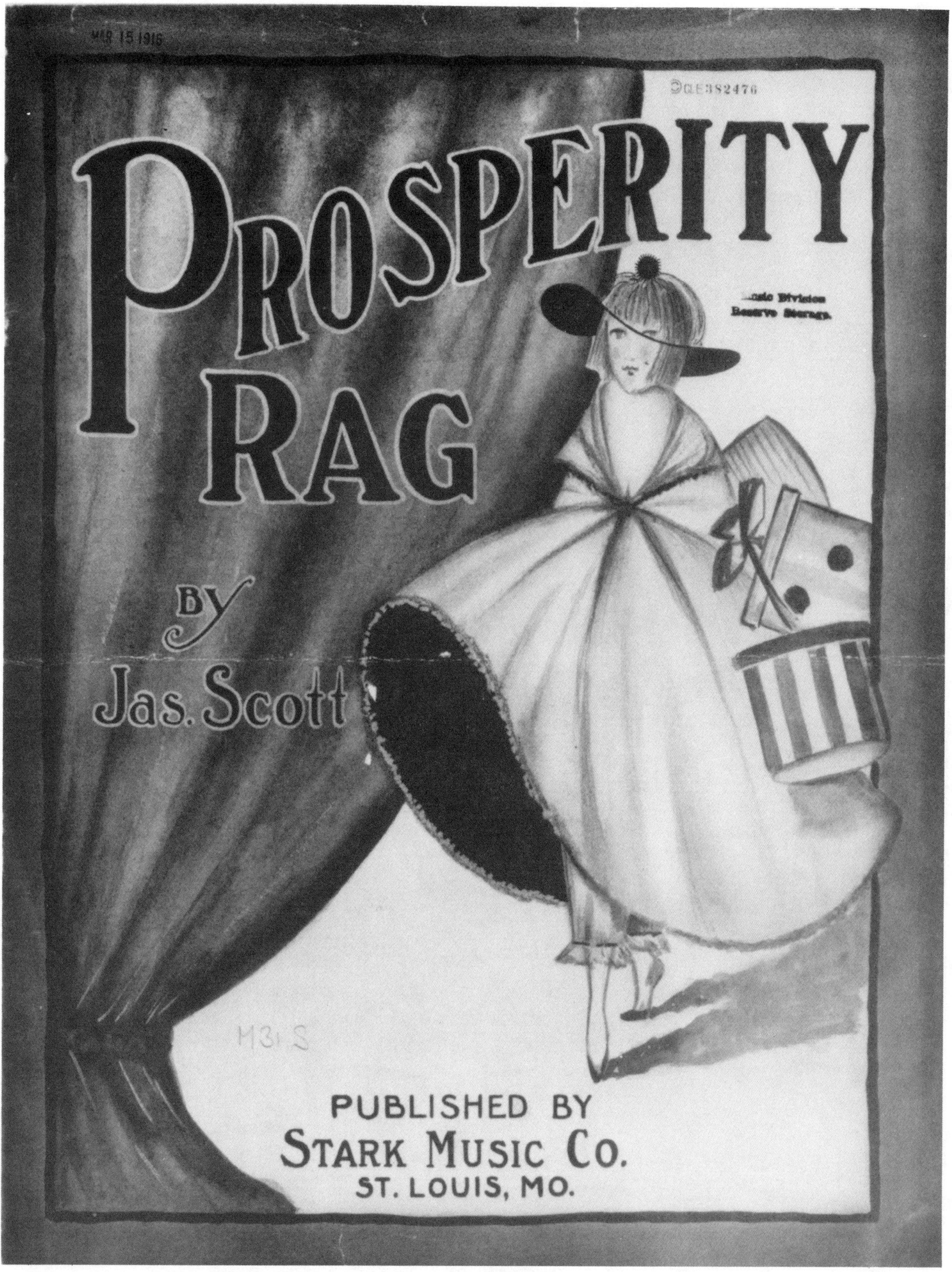
MAR 15 1916
©CLE382476
PROSPERITY
RAG
BY
Jas. Scott
M31 S
PUBLISHED BY
STARK MUSIC CO.
ST. LOUIS, MO.

Prosperity Rag

JAMES SCOTT

Efficiency Rag

JAMES SCOTT

Paramount Rag

JAMES SCOTT
Com. of Grace and Beauty Rag

DIXIE DIMPLES
Novelty Rag Fox Trot

By JAMES SCOTT
Composer of
"GRACE AND BEAUTY RAG" etc.

RAG SENTIMENTAL

By James Scott

Rag Sentimental

JAMES SCOTT

New Era Rag

JAS. SCOTT

Not too fast

Peace and Plenty Rag

JAMES SCOTT

TROUBADOUR RAG

By James Scott

Troubadour Rag

JAMES SCOTT

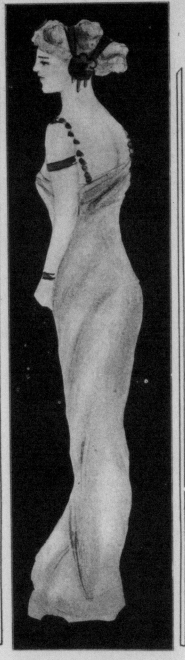

Modesty Rag

A CLASSIC

JAMES SCOTT
Composer of Frog Legs

PEGASUS

A CLASSIC RAG

JAMES SCOTT

Don't Jazz Me- Rag

(I'M MUSIC)

JAMES SCOTT

Not too fast

Victory Rag

JAMES SCOTT

BROADWAY RAG

A CLASSIC

JAMES SCOTT
Comp. of "Grace and Beauty" etc.

WALTZES

BY
JAMES SCOTT

PUBLISHED BY
STARK MUSIC CO.
NEW YORK AND ST. LOUIS

VALSE VENICE.

JAMES SCOTT.

Copyright, **1909**, by Stark Music Printing and Pub. Co.

HEARTS

LONGING

WALTZES

By JAMES SCOTT.

50

PUBLISHERS OF
RAGTIME THAT IS DIFFERENT
STARK MUSIC CO.
ST. LOUIS, MO.   127 EAST 23 ST.
NEW YORK.

HEARTS LONGING.

Waltzes.

JAMES SCOTT.
Com. of "Frog Legs."

THE SUFFRAGETTE
WALTZ
DEC 30 1914
Music Division
Reserve Storage
©CLE354906
By
James Scott
VOTES FOR WOMEN
M32,S
STARK MUSIC CO.
ST. LOUIS, MO.

THE SUFFRAGETTE.
VALSE.

JAMES SCOTT.

With expression.
Moderato.

Springtime of Love

VALSE

By JAMES SCOTT
Composer of
"Grace & Beauty Rag" etc.

Introduction Brilliant.

213   SPRINGTIME OF LOVE

Springtime of Love **3**

 SONGS

She's my Girl from Anaconda.

Words by
C. R. DUMARS.

Music by
JAMES SCOTT.

Some-time a - go I start-ed out to seek my
I knew that I would have to go to work and

for - tune,　Out in the west,　the Gol-den West.　I'd of - ten
hus - tle　Out with the boys,　the min-ing boys　So Sue and

11
heard that mon - ey grew out there on bush - es,   I could not
I could go back home to New York Cit - y   to hear the

13   **15**
rest,   till I could test.   So in An - a - con - da in Mon - ta - na
noise,   the cit - y noise,   We had planned for wed - ding bells as soon as

17
I just made a start, and at once I met the Dear - est girl and
I could make a stake, and to go back East and live in ease for

mf   *p*

WORDS BY
C. R. DUMARS

MUSIC BY
JAMES SCOTT

PUBLISHED
BY
DUMARS GAMMON
MUSIC CO
CARTHAGE . MO

Sweetheart Time.

Words by
C. R. DUMARS.

Music by
JAMES SCOTT.

mine   Looks   fair - er   and   sweet - er   than   an -   y
spoon   My   Sweet - heart   and   I   had   that   eve -   ning

Rose   That   is   known far   the   sweet - est   of   all   that   grows   Her
planned   and   were   go - ing   up   town, just   to   hear   the   Brass   Band   Her

eyes   are   dark   brown and   her   hair   is   too   Her   teeth   are   like
moth - er   and   Fath - er   said   they'd   go   too   For   neith - er   had

Pearl, but   of   bet - ter   hue   She   looks   ve - ry   neat   and   is
an - y - thing   else   to   do   This   made her   so   mad   and made

so ve - ry sweet She is Joy - ful and nev - er gets blue.
me feel so bad for they made this bright night a hoo - doo.

CHORUS.

It was sweet - heart time when she

said I'm thine, If you ask my

Pa - pa and my ma - ma and they give their

Take Me Out To Lakeside

Words by
IDA MILLER

Music by
JAMES SCOTT

The Shimmie Shake

Words by
CLEOTA WILSON

Music by
JAMES SCOTT

CRITICAL COMMENTARY

The critical notes in this section report discrepancies between the edition and the original published version (the unique source) of each composition by James Scott. All reports describe the original version. Detailed discussions of interpretative problems concerning text, dynamics, and articulation and the rationale for certain editorial emendations are provided in the "Comments" sections.

Variant readings are located by strain and measure number (see Editorial Policy, under "Terminology"), voice (right hand or upper piano staff, left hand or lower piano staff, and vocal line in songs), and variously (sometimes in combination) by beat, note value, note, chord, octave, and so on. Pitch names are identified by the familiar system wherein c′ = middle C, c = the octave below middle C, c″ = the octave above middle C, and so on. The following abbreviations are also used: A (B, C, D) = A (B, C, D) strain, Int = interlude, Intro = introduction, Cr = composer credit, RH = right hand or upper piano staff, LH = left hand or lower piano staff, V = vocal line in songs, and m(m). = measure(s).

RAGS

A Summer Breeze

CRITICAL NOTES

A1:13	LH, beat 2, second octave, top note has ♯.
A1:14	LH, beat 2, second eighth, bottom note of chord has ♯.
B:8	RH, beat 2, third sixteenth, no ♮.
A2:6	RH, note 1, no continuation tie from last note of m. 5.
A2:13	LH, beat 2, second octave, top note has ♯.
Int:4	Single barline at end.
D:4	LH, beat 2, chord is quarter note, lacks flag.
D:7	RH, note 5 has ♮.
D:16a, 16b	LH, second octave is aligned with second sixteenth-note chord in RH.

COMMENTS

The f♮′ in Intro:2 (RH, beat 1, third sixteenth) is presumably correct, despite the cross relation with f♯ in the left hand.

The musical significance of the upward stem on e in the left-hand part of A1:3, 7, and 11 and A2:3 and 7 is obscure. Perhaps Scott or his publisher intended a series of upward stems to highlight the descending bass line F–E–D–C.

The f''' in B:8 (RH, beat 2, first sixteenth) may be a misprint for g'''.

The main rhythmic motive of the right hand in C could be notated more clearly as follows:

The dynamic marking in A1:13 probably applies to A2:13 as well.

The Fascinator

CRITICAL NOTES

A1:7	LH, octaves are beamed as two eighth notes.
A1:7–8	RH, no slurs on grace notes—emended after A2:7–8.
A1:10	RH, articulation appears as follows:

A1:16a	LH, beat 1, top note of octave (c') lacks ledger line.
B:16a	LH, beat 1, top note of octave (c') lacks ledger line.
B:16b	No "loco" indication (marking a return to original octave after repeating the strain an octave higher).
A2:5	LH, beat 1, second eighth, middle note of chord (c♯') lacks ledger line.
C:13	RH, first chord, second note from top has ♭.
D:11	RH, beat 2, chord (e♭'–a♮'–d♭') has extraneous upward stem.

COMMENTS

The right-hand chords in D:4 have an f' absent from the corresponding chords in D:12. Either reading is plausible.

No dynamic markings are given for A2, C, or D.

On the Pike

CRITICAL NOTES

Intro:2	LH, no rest.

A1:8	LH, beat 1, second eighth, no ♮s—emended after A2:8.
A1:14	LH, no rest.
B:16a	LH, note 1 is quarter note, lacks flag.
A2:1	Single barline at beginning; RH, grace notes, no slur.
A2:8	RH, beat 1, second sixteenth has ♮.
A2:14	LH, no rest.
A2:16	Single barline at end.
C:1	No repeat bar.
C:17	RH, beat 1, first chord, bottom note (c') lacks ledger line.
C:25	RH, beat 1, first chord, bottom note has ♮.
C:29	RH, ♮ before d' instead of b.

COMMENT

The double stems on beat 2 of Intro:2, A1:14, and A2:14 have been retained, although they may result from typographical error.

Frog Legs Rag

CRITICAL NOTES

A1:13	LH, beat 2, second eighth, ♭ before d' instead of c'.
A2:7	RH, note 3 has extraneous ledger line above it.
Int:1	RH, first chord, bottom note has ♮.
Int:2	RH, first chord, bottom and top notes have ♮; LH, note 3 has ♮.
Int:4	LH, beat 2, lower note is F.
C:3	RH, notes 3–4, no tie.
C:11	RH, notes 3–4, no tie.
D:12	LH, beat 2, second eighth, ♭ before a instead of g.

COMMENTS

For the trio or C strain of a ragtime piece, the composer usually modulates to the subdominant. In "Frog Legs Rag" Scott modulates instead to the dominant. Jasen and Tichenor have suggested that John Stark's reluctance to publish a section in the "difficult" key of G♭ may be responsible for this unusual feature.[1]

---

1. David A. Jasen and Trebor Jay Tichenor, *Rags and Ragtime: A Musical History* (New York: Seabury Press, 1978), 113.

The two appearances of the A strain differ in their dynamic markings. Strain A1 is marked *mf*, has a swell in measure 14, and ends *f* beginning with measure 15. Strain A2 begins *f* and has two swells in measures 6–7 and 8. In other rags where the dynamic levels of the A strains are dissimilar, the tendency is for A1 to have most of the information and A2 very little. It is possible that the expressive dynamics in A2:6–8 were meant in fact for A1:6–8, and mistakenly placed in the later strain. Were this to be the case, "Frog Legs Rag" would correspond more closely to the pattern in "Climax Rag" and "Don't Jazz Me—Rag," where A1 is marked *mf* with expressive dynamics, and A2 is neutrally marked *f*.

Slurs were probably intended over the first four sixteenth notes of A2:2, 4 (as in A1:2, 4).

Kansas City Rag

CRITICAL NOTES

A:16b	RH, no eighth rest.
B:2	LH, second eighth, top note of chord, no ♮—emended after B:10.
B:9	RH, beat 1, second sixteenth, no ♯.
C:8	Thin-thin double barline at end.
C:13	RH, beat 2, second sixteenth, upper note (a″) lacks ledger line.
C:14	LH, beat 2, first octave, lower note, no ♯.
Int:4	Thin-thick double barline at end.

Grace and Beauty

CRITICAL NOTES

A1:7	LH, beat 2, second eighth, top note of chord, no ♮.
B:12	RH, beamed as follows:

A2:8	LH, beat 1, first eighth, lower note is D♭, second eighth, top note of chord, no ♭—emended after A1:8.
A2:12	LH, beat 1, first eighth, no ♭s—emended after A1:12.
A2:14	RH, notes 3–5 are d♭″, e♭″, e♮″.
A2:16	LH, appears as follows—emended to correspond with A1:16:

C:5	RH, beat 1, tie ambiguously notated as slur between f″ and d♭″.
C:7	RH, note 4 is dyad b♭″–d♭‴.

COMMENTS

The basic rhythm of the D strain, found in measures 1–4 and 9–12, is notated no fewer than three different ways. All of these notations are plausible and result in the same sonority, and have therefore been retained in this edition.

A dynamic marking of *mf* for A2 (to correspond with A1) was probably intended, since all other dynamic markings correspond.

The presence of a slur over the ascending pentatonic passage in Intro:1 seems to indicate a similar legato articulation for related motivic material in A:1, 5, and 9.

The slur that connects the last left-hand eighth-note octave in A1:12 to the first eighth-note octave in A1:13 does not appear in A2:12–13. The slur over the last three sixteenth notes in the right hand of A1:14 does not appear in A2:14. The absence of these slurs in A2 was probably inadvertent.

Great Scott Rag

CRITICAL NOTES

Intro	Dynamic marking (*f*) from m. 1, beat 1.
A:6	RH, beat 1, second sixteenth, middle note of chord, no tie to sixteenth on beat 2.
B1:15	RH, beat 1, fourth sixteenth, bottom note of chord, no ♮, beat 2, last chord, middle note has ♮.
C:6	RH, beat 1, second sixteenth, middle note of chord, no ♮—emended after C:2.
C:7	LH, beat 2, last octave, no ♯s.
C:9	RH, fourth and fifth sixteenths, upper note is d‴.
C:15	RH, beat 1, second sixteenth, g″–b″.
B2:15	RH, beat 1, first and third sixteenths, top note of chord is c‴, beat 1, fourth sixteenth, bottom note of chord, no ♮, and middle note of chord lacks tie to beat 2, beat 2, last chord, middle note has ♮.
B2:16a	RH, no 8va.

COMMENTS

The two versions of the B strain—B1 in G major, B2 in C major—differ in a number of details. The slight change in melodic contour in measures 6–7, left hand, gives some idea of how variants in the bass line might be constructed and perhaps inserted ad lib. The differences in the voicing of the right-hand chords in measures 13–14, on the other hand, may result from Scott's adjusting of the chords to the higher register.

The A strain lacks a dynamic marking. Despite the marking of *f* for the Intro, the dynamic level of A should probably drop to *mf*—that is, the same level as B1 on its first appearance.

The marking *mp–f* in B1:16b applies to the C strain. It is likely that on its repetition, the C strain should be played *f* all the way through, ignoring the *mp* in C:5. The D strain, which lacks a dynamic marking, should continue at *f*.

The slurring in the A strain is internally inconsistent, as well as ambiguous in its indication of phrasing. The slur extending across the barline in A:9–10 suggests strongly that similar across-the-barline phrasing be used throughout the strain. The opening measures of the strain should probably be played as follows:

The Ragtime "Betty"

CRITICAL NOTES

A1:1	No repeat bar.
A1:5	RH, beat 1, third sixteenth, ♯ appears in fourth space; LH, beat 1, occupied by eighth-note octave and eighth rest.
A1:13	LH, beat 1, occupied by eighth-note octave and eighth rest, no indication "L.H."
A1:15	RH, lower voice, note 1, no ♮, beat 2, lower voice, two eighth notes (e♮′, e♭′)—emended after A2:15.
A2:2	RH, notes 4–5, no tie.
A2:4	RH, notes 4–5, no tie.
A2:5	LH, occupied by eighth-note octave, eighth rest, and quarter rest.
A2:6	RH, beat 2, third sixteenth, top note of chord, no ♮—emended after A1:6.
A2:13	LH, occupied by eighth-note octave, eighth rest, and quarter rest, no indication "L.H."
A2:15	LH, beat 2, second eighth is chord f–b♭–c′—emended after A1:15.
C:1	No repeat bar and no dash between dynamic markings.
C:13	RH, beat 2, second sixteenth, accidentals are reversed.
C:14	RH, beat 2, second sixteenth, top ♮ appears before middle note of chord.
C:15	RH, chord is g′–b♭′–d″–f″—emended after C:7—middle notes have slurs (ties) that extend to end of measure but not to C:16a.
C:16a	RH, beat 1, first eighth, no continuation slurs from C:15, beat 2, octaves are b♮′–b♮″, b♭′–b♭″.
C:16b	RH, beat 1, first eighth, middle notes of chord have continuation tie.
D:1	No repeat bar.
D:3	LH, beat 2, first eighth, top note of chord is f′—emended after D:11.
D:16b	RH, note 1, no continuation slur from D:15.

COMMENTS

"The Ragtime 'Betty'" is notable for the unusually high number of typographical errors: omitted or misplaced accidentals, notes placed too high or too low on the staff, and so forth.

Two otherwise identical measures, C:1 and C:9, differ in two details. The second right-hand octave in C:1 has an e♭″ that is absent from C:9, and the inner note of the next-to-last right-hand chord is g″ in C:1, e♭″ in C:9. The differences are of negligible musical importance and were probably unintentional. Since either reading is plausible, the discrepancies have been retained in the edition.

A dynamic marking of *p* is probably intended in A1:13, to correspond with A1:5. The crescendo marking in A1:14 would lead to a return to *mf* in A1:15. A2 has no dynamic markings. The dynamic markings for A1 probably apply.

The slurring for the main melodic material of the A strain is internally inconsistent, with some slurs covering only groups of four sixteenth notes (A1:1), others covering an entire measure (A1:11), and others omitted entirely (A2:10). It seems likely, in any case, that A:1–4 and A:9–12 should be phrased in two-measure groupings:

Slurs are lacking in B:6, beat 1, and B:12, beat 2 (cf. similar figuration in B:4, 8). The slur in C:10 should probably extend to the downbeat of C:11 (cf. C:2–3).

Sunburst Rag

CRITICAL NOTES

A1:1	No repeat bar.
A1:3	LH, beat 2, quarter rest.
A1:4	RH, beat 2, appears as follows—emended to correspond with A2:4:

	LH, beat 1, quarter rest.
A1:13	RH, grace notes, no slur.
A1:14	RH, upper voice, notes 4–5, no tie.
A1:16b	RH, no continuation slur from A1:15; RH and LH, single barline at end.
B1:1	No repeat bar.
B1:8	RH, beat 1, no upstemmed eighth note (cf. B1:14, B2:8, B2:14).
A2:1	Single barline at beginning.
A2:2	RH, lower voice, notes 2–3, no tie.
A2:3	LH, beat 2, quarter rest.
A2:4	LH, beat 1, quarter rest.
A2:12	LH, beat 2, last octave, no ♮s.
Int:2	RH, beat 2, eighth-note chord, top note has ♯.
Int:3–4	RH, no across-the-barline slurs.
C:4	RH, beat 1, first eighth, accidental is ♮, second eighth, top note of chord has ♯.
C:12	RH, beat 1, second eighth, top note of chord has ♯, beat 2, eighth-note chord is octave e′– e″, first sixteenth chord is octave e♭′–e♭″— emended after C:4.

COMMENTS
"Sunburst Rag" is particularly notable for the use of jazz "breaks" in the first and third strains (A:3–4, 7–8; C:7–8). These momentary disruptions of the normal ragtime texture

draw upon a vocabulary of stock formulas: descending chromatic chords (as in Scott Joplin's and Louis Chauvin's "Heliotrope Bouquet," B:7–8), bass "solos" (Scott's own "Hilarity Rag," A:15–16), and ascending chords (Jelly Roll Morton's "Grandpa's Spells," B:7–8).

An interesting example of (probably unconscious) self-borrowing may be seen in the close similarity of "Sunburst Rag," B:7–8, with "The Ragtime 'Betty'," C:2–3.

The first notes in the bass clef of A2:2 and A2:6 were probably intended to carry an upward stem, as in A1:2 and A1:6.

The slur over the descending eighth-note chords in A1:3–4 probably applies to A2:3–4 as well. Similarly, the slur connecting A1:15–16 probably applies to A2:15–16.

In B1 the slur over the first four sixteenths of the measure (as in B1:3, 9, 11, and 15) seems to have been inadvertently omitted in B1:1. In B2 all such slurs are lacking.

In the original published text, the slurs connecting the right-hand chords in Int:3–4 were absent. They have been added because of the obvious parallel with the preceding measure combined with the presence of the slur in the left hand, and because of their importance in indicating phrasing across the barline.

Although staccato marks appear over only the first three chords in the ascending sequence in C:7, it is likely that the entire passage, up through the downbeat of C:8, should be played staccato.

Hilarity Rag

CRITICAL NOTES

A:10	RH, beat 2, second chord is f′–d♭″–f″— emended after A:2.
A:16b	Single barline at end.
B:1	No repeat bar.
B:11	RH, sixteenth chords are octave e♭″–e♭‴— emended after B:3.
C:1	No repeat bar.
D:1	No repeat bar, thin-thin double barline only.
D:15	LH, beats 1 and 2, second eighth, chord is a♭– b♭–c′—emended after C:15.

COMMENT
The fact that no dynamic marking above *mf* appears in "Hilarity Rag" should be noted; despite its pianistic brilliance, this is not a piece to be played loudly.

Ophelia Rag

CRITICAL NOTES

Cr	"Com. of 'Frogg Legs.'"
Intro:4	RH, beat 1, eighth rest.
A:1	No repeat bar.
A:16a	RH, beat 1, note (c′) lacks ledger line.
A:16b	RH, beat 1, d′, beat 2, first eighth, chord is g′–c″–e″–g″—emended after B:16a—second eighth, chord is dyad a′–f♯″—emended after B:16a.
B1:14	LH, beat 1, second eighth, middle note of chord, no ♮—emended after B2:14.
C:1	No repeat bar.
C:4	RH, beat 2, redundant eighth rest above staff.
C:16a	RH, grace notes, lack ledger lines and slurs.
B2:1	RH, beat 1, bottom note of chord is f′—emended after B1:1.
B2:7	RH, beat 2, rhythm is two sixteenths and eighth—emended after B1:7.
B2:9	RH, beat 1, bottom note of chord is f′—emended after B1:9.
B2:15	LH, last note (to m. 16, beat 1), no tie.

COMMENTS

The cover design is by Clare Victor Dwiggins (1874–1959), creator of the cartoon strip "Ophelia Bump." Dwiggins drew many fine comic strips in addition to "Ophelia," among them "School Days," "Tom Sawyer and Huck Finn," and "Nipper." His major theme was boyhood in rural America at the turn of the century.

The original reading of the two chords immediately preceding the downbeat of B (A1:16b), although plausible in its own right, has been discarded in favor of the voicing heard in every other appearance (see B1:16a, C:16b, and m. 8 of both B1 and B2, where the voicing of the chord on beat 2 is disguised by the E tied over from the previous beat).

The chord on the downbeat of B2:1 and 9 in the original outlined an octave f′–f″ instead of the minor seventh g′–f″ heard in B1. This variant has been rejected as less plausible on the grounds that the f′ would overlap with the chords in the left hand.

The crescendo in A:7–8 should probably begin *p*, in order not to exceed the dynamic marking of *mf* in A:9. A crescendo marking to increase the volume from *p* in C:1 to *mf* in C:3 was probably omitted. The same markings probably apply to C:9–11.

The slurring in the left hand of C is confusing and internally inconsistent. The composer clearly used slurs to highlight the motive (🎵); and in cases where the slur exists over only the first three sixteenth notes (e.g., C:8), it should be understood to extend to the following downbeat. At the same time, the entire single-note left-hand passage in C:1–3 (including the anacrusis in Int:4), appearing again in C:8–11, seems to be one long legato phrase. The logical result is the overlapping slurs of C:10.

The Princess Rag

CRITICAL NOTES

Cr	"Comp. of Frog Leggs Rag."
Intro:3	RH, note 4 has ♮.
A:1	No repeat bar.
B1:1	No repeat bar.
B1:15	LH, notes 3–4, no tie.
B1:16b	RH and LH, beat 2, no eighth rest.
C:1	No repeat bar.
C:7	LH, beat 2, second octave, top note has ♮.
B2:11	LH, beats 1 and 2, first eighth, no upward stem—emended after B1:11.
B2:13	LH, beat 1, first eighth, no upward stem—emended after B1:13.

COMMENTS

The rhythmic pattern that dominates the A strain (🎵) is derived from the characteristic cakewalk figure (🎵) as A1:15 makes clear. Other details in the piece—sustained notes with offbeat accompaniment (B:3) or countermelodies (C:1–2) and the oscillating chromatic figure in B:4—suggest a closer relationship with the concert march than is usual with the Scott rags.

The opening measure of the A strain recalls the popular melody usually known as "I Thought I Heard Buddy Bolden Say," published in 1904 as "St. Louis Tickle" by Barney and Seymore. Trebor Jay Tichenor notes that the melody was "well known in Missouri."[2]

The right-hand chord on beat 1 of B1:15 differs slightly from the chord on beat 1 of B2:15. One or the other is prob-

2. Trebor Jay Tichenor, comp., *Ragtime Rarities: Complete Original Music for 63 Piano Rags* (New York: Dover Publications, 1975), viii.

ably a misprint, but which is correct is impossible to determine on the basis of internal evidence. An obvious precedent for the reading in B1 is the chord on beat 1 of B1:7; but B2 corresponds more closely to the tendency for right-hand chords in B to include an octave.

The dynamic marking for B1 (*f*) probably applies to B2 as well.

Slurs over beat 2 of A:11, left hand, and A:13, right hand (as in A:3 and A:5, respectively), were probably inadvertently omitted. The slur over the last three sixteenth notes in the left hand of B1:5 should extend to the downbeat of B1:6 (as in B1:13–14).

Slurs and accent marks in B2 should probably correspond with B1. Slurs are lacking in B2:6, 8, and 14 (right hand) and in B2:13–14 (left hand). Accent marks are lacking on the downbeats of B2:5, 7, and 13 (right hand).

Quality

CRITICAL NOTES

A1:3, 5, 7	RH, beat 1, no upward stem—emended after A2:5, 7, and 11.
A1:8	RH, beat 2, second note of triplet, no ♭.
A1:11	RH, beat 1, no upward stem—emended after A2:5, 7, and 11.
B1:2	LH, beat 1, second eighth, chord includes b♭—emended after B2:2.
B1:9	LH, beat 1, second eighth, chord includes b♭.
A2:3	RH, beat 1, no upward stem.
A2:7	RH, beat 1, second eighth, chord includes a♭″—emended after A1:7.
A2:8	RH, beat 2, second note of triplet, no ♭.
A2:14	RH, beat 2, second chord, second note from top, no ♭.
C:1	No repeat bar.
C:2, 4	RH, 8va brackets from C:1, 3, respectively.
C:15	RH, beat 1, first chord, middle note, no ♮, second chord, second note from top has ♮.
C:16a	No numeral "1."
C:16b	No numeral "2."
Int:4	RH, beat 1, octave, no ♮s.
B2:6	RH, beat 1, second eighth, no ♮s.
B2:13	RH, beat 2, second sixteenth and eighth, no tie.
B2:14	RH, beat 2, second sixteenth and eighth, no tie.

COMMENTS

Double stems have been added to the right-hand F in measures 3, 5, 7, and 11 of A1 to correspond not only with most of the A2 strain but also with the similar figuration in the B strain of "Honey Moon Rag" (B:5–8).

In the first appearance of the B strain, two of the left-hand dominant chords (B1:2, 9) have four notes in place of the three-note chord used elsewhere. For consistency the extra note in these two chords has been deleted.

A significant textual change was made in the C strain. In the original the ottava brackets appear over C:1 and C:3. This is inconsistent not only with Scott's usual practice (in which repetition of material an octave higher is always the "response," not the "call") but also with the way the same material is presented in C:9–12. Accordingly, the brackets have been moved to C:2 and C:4.

The dynamic marking for A2 is lacking. Either a return to *mf* (as in the first appearance of A1) or a continuation of the *f* of B1 (on its second appearance) seems appropriate.

Ragtime Oriole

CRITICAL NOTES

Intro:1	LH, anacrusis, no sixteenth rest.
Intro:2	RH, lower voice, note 3, quarter note; LH, occupied by quarter rest, eighth rest, and eighth-note octave.
Intro:4	Single barline at end.
A1:1	No repeat bar.
A1:11	RH, notes 1–6, no fingering—added after A2:11.
A1:14	RH, lower voice, note 3, quarter note; LH, occupied by quarter rest, eighth rest, and eighth-note octave.
A1:16b	RH, beat 2, second eighth, chord includes c″—emended after B:16a.
B:15	LH, beat 2, second eighth, top note of chord, no ♭.
A2:7	RH, beat 2, second sixteenth, extraneous ledger line above top note; LH, beat 2, first eighth is d♭ only—emended after A1:7.
A2:10	LH, beat 2, first eighth, no ♮s—emended after A1:10.
A2:13	RH, no indications "L.H." and "R.H."
A2:14	RH, lower voice, beat 2, occupied by eighth note and eighth rest; LH, occupied by quarter rest, eighth rest, and eighth-note octave.

A2:16	Thin-thin double barline at end.
C:1	No repeat bar.
C:4	RH, second and third chords, bottom note is b♭′—emended after C:12.
D:2, 10	RH, second sixteenth, ♮ from first sixteenth.
D:16b	Marked "D.C. 𝄋 to Fine."; thin-thick double barline at end.

COMMENTS

The original text has a four-note chord, including c″, in A1:16b. This c″ has been deleted to correspond with B:16a. In all other instances in which a similar chord has c″ (B:4, B:8), the c″ resolves in the next measure to d♭″. B:1 lacks such as d♭″.

"Ragtime Oriole" is a unique instance in the Scott repertory of the return to the opening strain at the end of a piece (perhaps because the D strain leaves an inconclusive impression).

The dynamic marking for A2 is lacking. A return to the *mf* of A1 seems appropriate.

The slurring for Intro:1–4—the distinctive "break" that recurs in A1:13–16 and A2:13–16—is particularly inconsistent. Intro:3 lacks the slur over the first four sixteenth notes found in A1:15 and A2:15. A1:12–13 and A2:12–13 lack the slur found connecting the first three sixteenth notes of the Intro to the downbeat of Intro:1. A1:15 lacks the slur on the first two sixteenth notes of beat 2 found in Intro:3 and A2:15. A2:15–16 lacks the slur in the right hand connecting d♭′ and c′ found in Intro:3–4 and A1:15–16.

The existing slurring does not seem to capture adequately the polyrhythmic quality of the passage, with its additive rhythm of 3 + 3 + 2. One possible alternate reading is as follows:

It seems very likely that an additional slur was intended for the middle two notes of D:1, 3, and 5 (see below). The slurring in these measures should be understood to apply to succeeding measures (D:7, 9, 11, 13):

Climax Rag

CRITICAL NOTES

Intro:1	LH, anacrusis, no sixteenth rest.
Intro:2	LH, notated an octave higher (i.e., identical with RH); no clef change before m. 3.
Intro:4	Single barline at end.
A1:1	No repeat bar.
A1:12	RH, beat 1, second chord does not include c″—emended after A1:4, 8.
A1:14	RH, beat 1, first chord, top note, no ♮.
B1:1	No repeat bar.
B1:16b	Single barline at end.
A2:2	RH, note 3 (a″) lacks ledger line; LH, note 3, no ♮.
A2:5	LH, beat 1, second eighth, chord is g–b♭–f′, beat 2, second eighth, top note of chord is f′.
C:1	No repeat bar.
C:2	LH, note 1, no cautionary ♭—emended after C:6, 10.
C:11	RH, beat 2, second sixteenth and eighth, no tie.
C:16a	RH, beat 2, last note has ♯—emended after C:4, 8.
B2:10	RH, beat 1, chord does not include f′—emended after B2:2.

COMMENTS

In A1:14 a natural has been added to the top note of the first chord on the grounds that a tonicization of E♭ major has taken place in the previous measure, and a reversion to d♭‴ on the downbeat of measure 14 seems unlikely.

One discrepancy between the two appearances of the B strain should be noted: the sixteenth-note run in the right hand of B2:4 does not correspond with B1:4. The most plausible explanation is that B2:4 was copied by mistake from B1:12 or B2:12. The performer may therefore wish to substitute the diatonic passage from the B1 strain for the chromatic version in B2. But since either reading makes sense, the original text has been retained.

With "Climax Rag" Scott began the technique of composing different endings for the A strain on each of its two appearances. The first ending closes on the dominant, while the second comes to rest on the tonic.

Although crescendo and decrescendo markings in measures 3–4, 5–6, and 7–8 of the A strain are found only in

A1, the use of these swells to highlight the call-and-response phrasing in corresponding measures of A2 seems appropriate.

Slurring in B1 and B2 is internally inconsistent. Although most of the slurs cover only the group of six sixteenth notes, it seems likely that all of the slurs were meant to extend to the downbeat of the following measure, as in B1:4–5 and Int:4–B2:1. Similar slurs have been omitted entirely in B1:2–3, 8–9, 10–11, 12–13; and B2:4–5.

Evergreen Rag

CRITICAL NOTES

A:1	No repeat bar.
A:13	LH, beat 2, second eighth, middle note of chord has ♮.
B1:4	RH, beat 2, second sixteenth includes d″— emended after B1:12.
C:1	No repeat bar.
Int:4	Single barline at end.

COMMENTS

The rhythm in the left hand of the B strain (mm. 5, 7, and 13) is given variously as:

It is entirely possible that only one version is correct and that version C, especially, is an error. But since that "error" is repeated in both the B1 and B2 strains, it cannot be ruled out as a rhythmic variant.

Other minor discrepancies in the B strain involve two equally plausible variants. The left-hand octave D–d in measure 8 is a quarter note in B1 and an eighth note in B2. The last chord in the right hand of measure 6 is g″–c♯‴–e‴ in B1 and g″–a″–c♯‴ in B2. The right-hand chord on beat 1 of measure 12 has a lowest note of d″ in B1 and e″ in B2. In each case, no internal evidence supports one reading over the other.

In the Trio the descending bass line in C:9–10 is highlighted with accent marks. Similar marks were probably intended over the f on beat 2 of C:11, which has a double stem, and possibly the e on beat 1 of C:12.

A dynamic level of *mf* or below would seem to be indicated in B:1, to avoid exceeding the dynamic level of *f* in

B:3. The crescendo in B:1–3 is probably intended for B:9–11 as well.

The right-hand slur in B1:1–3 presumably applies to B1:9–11, B2:1–3, and B2:9–11 as well.

Accent marks were probably inadvertently omitted in B1:5 (LH, beat 1, second eighth), B1:6 (LH, beat 1), and B2:13 (RH, beat 2).

Honey Moon Rag

CRITICAL NOTES

A1:1	No repeat bar.
A1:7	RH, beat 1, second chord, top note, no ♭.
A1:8	RH, beat 1, second chord, top note, no ♭.
B:1	No repeat bar.
A2:13	LH, beat 2, first eighth, top note of chord is g′.
C:1	No repeat bar.
C:2, 10	RH, beat 1, fourth sixteenth, ♯ from middle note of first sixteenth.
Int2:1	LH, beat 1, last sixteenth, bottom note of chord has ♮.
Int2:2	LH, beat 1, last sixteenth, bottom note of chord has ♮.
B2:1	No repeat bar.

COMMENTS

The decrease in volume to *mf* in B1:4–5, followed by a return to *f* in B1:9, probably applies to the corresponding measures in B2, where such markings are lacking.

The accent marks on the left-hand octaves in the A strain found in A1:1, 10–11, and 16 presumably apply wherever the unaccompanied octave figure occurs.

Prosperity Rag

CRITICAL NOTES

A1:1	No repeat bar.
A1:15	RH, beat 1, no lower slur.
B1:1 .	No repeat bar.
B1:16a–b	RH, no 8va (ends at m. 15).
A2:15	RH, beat 1, no slurs.
Int1:2	LH, no clef change.
Int1:3	RH, beat 2, first chord, second note from top has ♭; LH, beat 1, fourth sixteenth, both notes have ♭.

C:5   RH, beat 2, fourth sixteenth, no ties to first chord in m. 6.

C:7   RH, beat 2, last chord, no ♮s; LH, beat 1, second eighth, top note of chord, no ♮.

B2:5   LH, beat 1, second eighth, top note of chord, no ♮.

B2:13   LH, beat 1, first eighth, no ♮s.

COMMENTS

It should be noted that the b″ in the right hand of A:3 (note 2) remains flat, despite the cross-relation with the b♮ in the left hand (beat 1, second eighth).

The A strain of "Prosperity Rag" appears to be modeled directly on the A strain of "Grace and Beauty," with the harmonic progression differing only in the last four-bar phrase.

The sequence of dynamic markings in A2 is illogical: beginning *f*, crescendoing twice in A2:13–14 to *f* in A2:15. It is possible that the initial dynamic marking should be *mf*, as in A1.

The accent marks on the first two chords of Int2:1 suggest that the first two chords of Int2:2, and possibly the downbeat of Int2:3, be similarly accented.

Slurs have been added in A1:15 and A2:15, where apparently omitted, to clarify the two-note motive in the right hand of A:13–15:

Efficiency Rag

CRITICAL NOTES

B1:1   No repeat bar.

B1:8   LH, bass clef with treble-clef cue at beginning of staff.

Int:1–3   LH, notes 2–3, no tie.

C:1–3, 5–6   RH, beat 1, second chord, second note from bottom lacks tie to first chord on beat 2.

C:11   RH, beat 2, occupied by three eighth-note octaves.

B2:1–2   RH, no 8va mark—emended after B1:1–2.

COMMENTS

In B1:6 the second left-hand octave is A–a—the sixth degree of the scale in C major. In B2:6 the same passage has C–c—the fifth degree in the new key of F major. This discrepancy

is more likely a conscious variation in the melodic contour of the bass line than a typographical error.

The discrepancy between the highest octave in C:1–2 and C:5–6—g″–g‴ in the former, f″–f‴ in the latter—is presumably also a conscious variation.

The crescendo and decrescendo marks in Intro:1–3 probably apply to A1:13–15 (which has decrescendo only), B1:13–15, A2:13–15, and B2:13–15. The crescendo in Intro:4 probably applies to A1:16a and B1:16b. The crescendo in A1:8 probably applies to A2:8. The crescendo and decrescendo in B1:7–8 probably applies to B2:7–8.

In A1:16a only the right-hand chords are accented; in B2:16b only the left-hand octaves are accented. In all probability both the right-hand chords and left-hand octaves should be accented, following Intro:4.

The accent mark on the second right-hand chord in A1:1 is lacking in the corresponding measure of A2.

The last three sixteenth notes of B2:8, left hand, should probably be connected by a slur to the downbeat of B2:9 (as in the corresponding measures of B1).

Paramount Rag

CRITICAL NOTES

Intro:4   RH, beat 2, second sixteenth, no ♮.

A:1   No repeat bar; RH, beat 2, third sixteenth, top note, no ♭.

A:3   RH, beat 2, third sixteenth, top note, no ♭.

A:4   RH, beat 1, no slurs.

A:9   RH, beat 2, first sixteenth, bottom note, no ♮, third sixteenth, top note, no ♭.

A:10   RH, beat 1, no lower slur.

A:11   RH, beat 2, first sixteenth, bottom note, no ♮, third sixteenth, top note, no ♭.

A:12   RH, beat 1, no slurs.

A:16a   RH, beat 2, second sixteenth, no ♮.

B:1   No repeat bar.

B:2   RH, beat 2, first sixteenth, middle note of chord, no ♭.

B:4   RH, beat 2, second sixteenth, no ♮.

B:10   RH, beat 2, first sixteenth, middle note of chord, no ♭.

B:11   RH, beat 1, bottom note of chord, no ♭.

B:12   RH, beat 2, second sixteenth, no ♮.

B:15   RH, beat 1, first sixteenth, top note of chord, no ♮.

C:1   No repeat bar.

C:3   LH, beat 2, second eighth, middle note of chord is c′.

C:9   LH, beat 1, first eighth, bottom note (D) lacks ledger line.

C:13   LH, beat 1, first eighth, bottom note, no ♮, beat 2, second eighth, top note has ♮.

D:7   RH, beat 1, third chord, next to lowest note, no ♭.

D:12   RH, beat 1, first sixteenth, lower note is e♭′.

COMMENTS

Jasen and Tichenor speculate that Scott's familiarity with the theater organ may explain the unusually large leaps in A:1, 3, 9, and 11: "These dramatic register shifts seem difficult for piano, but are much easier for a multiple-keyboard theater organ such as [the] one used by Scott. Instead of having to move quickly in a horizontal movement up and down the piano, one moves vertically, minimizing actual physical movements."[3]

The discrepancy between A:15 and B:15 is undoubtedly the result of typographical error. Unfortunately, it is difficult to determine which of several possibilities may be correct. At issue is the resolution of d♮″ to d♭″, corresponding to the change of harmony from B♭7 (II⁷) to E♭7 (V⁷). In A:15 the d♮″ does not resolve to d♭″ until the last chord of the measure. The resulting dissonance is somewhat jarring, but no less so than several other passages in Scott's output (including the f′–f♭ clash in B:5 of this rag). The passage in B:15, with the resolution to d♭ coming much closer to the change of harmony, sounds much more idiomatic. The legitimacy of B:15, however, is compromised by the absence of a natural on d″ on beat 1, an obvious typographical error. The reading in B:15 (with the missing natural sign added) is probably the intended text; but because of the ambiguities outlined above, both readings have been retained in this edition.

The first right-hand octave in A:14 should probably have c″ as in A:6, but there is insufficient evidence to decide between the two voicings.

The double-stemmed notes on beat 1 of C:1, 2, 5, 9, and 10 should probably be sustained no longer than an eighth note.

The last chord of the piece, marked "8," is actually two

---

3. Jasen and Tichenor, *Rags and Ragtime*, 118–19.

octaves higher than written because the entire strain is to be played ottava.

Slurs connecting f♯′–c″ to g′–b♭′ in A:2 were lacking, in whole or in part, in corresponding passages in A:4, 10, and 12. These slurs have been added in this edition.

Dixie Dimples

CRITICAL NOTES

Intro:1   RH, anacrusis, first dyad is eighth note; LH, anacrusis, first rest is eighth rest.

Intro:1   RH, lower voice, note 2 is quarter note.

A1:5   No dynamic marking—added after A2:5, A3:5; RH, upper voice, note 2 is e‴— emended after Intro:1.

B:2   RH, upper voice, note 6 has ♯.

B:4   RH, upper voice, note 3 is eighth note, lacks dot.

A2:1   RH, upper voice, note 4 (a″) lacks ledger line.

C:15   RH, upper voice, note 4 is b♭″.

A3:16   Thin-thin double barline at end.

COMMENTS

In its consistent use of dotted rhythms, its use of "common time" meter, its designation (on the cover) "Novelty Rag or Fox Trot," and its restrained pianistic technique, "Dixie Dimples" is an anomaly in the Scott repertoire. Certain passages are borrowed from other rags: Intro:1–2 and A:4–5 draw upon C:1–2 of "Climax Rag," while the B strain of "Dixie Dimples" strongly resembles the B strain of "Paramount Rag."

A decrease in dynamic level to *mp* is marked in measure 5 of both A2 and A3. No such indication appears in A1 in the original text. Because the three appearances of the A strain are otherwise identical, the marking of *mp* has been added to A1:5 in this edition.

Rag Sentimental

CRITICAL NOTES

A1:3   RH, beat 2, third sixteenth, second note from bottom of chord has ♮.

A1:7   LH, beat 2, second octave, top note has ♯.

A1:8   RH, beat 2, third sixteenth, top note of chord, no ♮.

A1:11   RH, beat 2, third sixteenth, second note from bottom of chord has ♮.

A1:15   RH and LH, no ties.

B:1   No repeat bar.

A2:1   RH, beat 2, third sixteenth, second note from bottom of chord has ♮.

A2:7   LH, beat 2, second octave, top note has ♯.

A2:8   RH, beat 2, third sixteenth, top note of chord, no ♮.

A2:9   RH, beat 2, third sixteenth, second note from bottom of chord has ♮.

A2:12   RH, beat 2, second eighth, middle note of chord, no ♭.

A2:15   RH, lower voice, note 7, no ♭; LH, beat 2, second eighth, second note from bottom of chord, no ♭.

C:4   RH, beat 1, third chord, and beat 2, first sixteenth, middle note of chord is e″—emended after C:8, 12.

C:9   RH, beat 2, no eighth rest—emended after C:1.

D:1   No repeat bar.

D:9   RH, beat 2, first and second sixteenths, no tie on f″.

D:16a   RH, beat 2, notes 1–3, ottava.

D:16a–b   RH, beat 1, chord is c′–a♭′–c″.

COMMENTS

Edward Berlin has recently noted the striking resemblance between A:1–4 and the initial Allegro passage in the first movement of Beethoven's Piano Sonata in D Minor, op. 31, no. 2—the sort of "standard repertory" that Scott may well have been exposed to in his youth.[4]

The discrepancy in the left-hand chords in D:1, 9 is probably unintentional. The performer may wish to substitute the chords in D:9 for the text in D:1.

The right-hand chord on beat 2 of D:6 (second eighth) is unusual. It is possible that Scott intended the descending inner voice to continue from e″ to d″, creating a dominant triad instead of the more ambiguous chord that stands in its place.

The chord on beat 1 of D:16a and 16b in the origi-

4. Edward A. Berlin, *Reflections and Research on Ragtime*, I.S.A.M. Monographs, no. 24 (Brooklyn, N.Y.: Institute for Studies in American Music, 1987), 14–15.

nal—c′–a♭′–c″—is extremely unlikely, since it fails to provide a perfect authentic cadence for the end of the strain (and the rag). The chord c′–e♭′–a♭′ has been put in its place.

The crescendo and decrescendo markings in A2:5–6 and A2:7–8 probably apply to the corresponding measures of A1.

New Era Rag

CRITICAL NOTES

B1:1   Thin-thin double barline at beginning, no repeat bar.

B1:3   RH, beat 2, occupied by sixteenth, eighth, sixteenth—emended after B1:1 and B2:3.

B1:4   RH, beat 1, third chord, middle notes, no ties to chord on beat 2.

B1:10   RH, beat 2, second sixteenth, no tie to top note of eighth-note chord.

B1:11   RH, beat 2, second sixteenth, no tie to top note of eighth-note chord.

B1:14   RH, beat 1, third chord, middle notes, no tie to chord on beat 2.

A2:8   RH, beat 1, second chord, bottom note is e″—emended after A1:4, 8.

C:1   No repeat bar.

C:2   RH, beat 1, first chord, second note from top, no ♭—emended after C:10.

C:7   RH, beat 2, first chord, top note, no ♮.

C:11   RH, beat 2, second chord, bottom note has ♯.

C:16b   RH, beat 2, chord is d″–f″–d‴.

B2:15   RH, beat 1, fourth sixteenth, bottom note of chord is d″, beat 2, first and second chords, bottom note is d″—all three chords emended after B1:15.

COMMENTS

The chord on beat 2 of C:16b in the original—d″–f″–d‴—is extremely unlikely because it fails to provide a perfect authentic cadence for the end of the strain. It has been replaced by b♭′–d″–b♭″.

The crescendo marking in C:3 probably applies to the similar passage in C:11.

The descending arpeggio in the B strain is provided with slurs only in B1:9, but legato articulation is probably intended for similar material throughout both appearances of the strain. The slur in the left hand of A2:12 is lacking in A1:12.

Peace and Plenty Rag

CRITICAL NOTES

Intro:1	RH, anacrusis, eighth rest before first chord.
A1:1	No repeat bar.
A1:14	RH, beat 1, small eighth note is a″.
B:1	No repeat bar.
B:5	RH, beat 1, first chord, top note is a‴— emended after B:13.
B:16a	RH, beat 2, first chord, bottom note is g′— emended after A1:16b and B:8.
B:16b	RH, beat 2, first chord, middle note is d″— emended after Intro:4, A1:8, A1:16a, and A2:8—second chord, middle note is d♯″— emended after Intro:4, A1:8, A:16a, and A2:8.
A2:2	RH, beat 1, first chord, top note is g″— emended after A1:2.
A2:11	RH, beat 1, second chord, ♯ from middle note.
A2:15	LH, beat 1, second chord, bottom note is f♮.
Int1:1	Single barline and no change of key signature at beginning.
C:1	No segno.
C:11	RH, beat 1, third chord, second note from bottom, no tie to first chord on beat 2.
C:15a, 15b	RH, second chord, next to top note has ♭.
C:16b	Thin-thin double barline at end.
Int2:12	Thin-thick double barline at end.

COMMENTS

Three otherwise identical measures in A1 and B differ in one small detail. Both A1:16b and B:8 have a′ as the bottom note of the first right-hand chord on beat 2, while the same chord in B:16a has g′. Although either reading is musically plausible (the second reading is slightly more dissonant), the weight of evidence supports the version with the a′.

A similar situation arises with the three right-hand chords serving as the pickup to the A strain. The reading in B:16b differs substantially from other appearances of the same material in Intro:4, A1:8, A1:16a, and A2:8. The weight of evidence supports the conclusion that the variants in B:16b are the result of typographical error.

The sequence of dynamics in the first half of the rag is illogical and confusing. The Intro, which is marked *f*, leads with a crescendo into A1, marked *mf*. It is possible that a decrease in volume in the Intro is expected to accompany the drop in register by Intro:3, or that the crescendo beginning in Intro:4 is simply meant to start at a lower volume level. Less easy to explain is the decrescendo leading from the *mf* of A1 into B, marked *f*. Since B is typically louder than A in Scott's rags, the dynamic marking of *f* seems genuine. It is possible that a decrescendo was mistakenly substituted for a crescendo in A1:16b.

Dynamic markings are entirely lacking in the first and second endings of B and throughout A2.

Given the consistency of slurring in C:2–3, 4–5, and 5–6, it is likely that the slurs in Int1:1, which cover the last three sixteenth notes of the measure, are intended to reach the following downbeat and that similar motives in Int1:2–3 and Int2:9–10 and 10–11 were meant to be slurred.

Troubadour Rag

CRITICAL NOTES

A1:1	No repeat bar.
A1:10	RH, beat 2, first chord, middle note, no ♮.
A1:11	RH, beat 1, first sixteenth, bottom and top notes of chord have ♮, third sixteenth, no ♮.
A2:11	RH, beat 1, third sixteenth, ♮ from beat 2, first sixteenth.
A2:14	RH, beat 2, occupied by two sixteenth-note chords (f♮″–a♭″–f♮‴), tied, and eighth rest; LH, beat 2, quarter-note octave (BB♮–B♮).
Int:3	RH, beat 1, first sixteenth, ♯ from bottom note of chord.
D:1	Thin-thin double barline at beginning, no repeat bar.
D:13	RH, beat 2, second chord, middle note has ♮.

COMMENTS

In D:10 the middle note of the right-hand chord on beat 2 was probably meant to be f♯″, as in D:2, rather than a♭″.

The dynamic marking for A2 is lacking; a return to the original dynamic level of *mf* seems appropriate.

The slurs for the ascending motive in A1:1, 3, and 9 are lacking in the corresponding measures of A2. It is likely, in any case, that the phrases should be longer—covering at least the two-measure units that the melodic line falls into in A1:1–2, 3–4.

The accent marks on the left-hand octave eighth note in B:16b and A1:16a undoubtedly apply to the anacrusis to A1:1 as well.

Modesty Rag

CRITICAL NOTES

A1:14	LH, beat 1, second eighth, top note of chord has ♯.
A2:15	LH, beat 2, second eighth, top note of chord, no ♮.
C:5	RH, lower voice, beat 2, second eighth, lower note, no ♮.
C:15	LH, beat 1, second eighth, middle note of chord, no ♯, beat 2, second eighth, top note of chord, no ♮.
B2:10	RH, beat 2, eighth, no d″—emended after B2:2.
B2:15	RH, beat 2, lower voice, note 1 is eighth note, lacks dot; LH, beat 1, second eighth, middle note of chord, no ♯, beat 2, second eighth, top note of chord, no ♮.

COMMENTS

The chords in Intro:1–2 may be divided between right and left hands.

In A1:3, 11 the right-hand chord on beat 1 is d′–f♯′–c″. In the same measures of A2, the chord lacks the d′. There is no internal evidence to support one version over the other.

In B1:6 the first left-hand octave on beat 2 is D–d; in B2:6 it is E–e. This is probably a conscious variation in the bass line rather than a misprint.

In B1:1, B1:9, B2:1, and B2:9, the right-hand note on beat 2 has an upper quarter-note stem. It seems unlikely that this notation is meant to be taken literally, since sustaining the f♯′ through the diminished seventh chord in the remainder of the measure would result in an unpleasant and uncharacteristic dissonance. The upper stem probably serves simply to emphasize the ascending four-note chromatic motive and the characteristic rhythmic gesture of four sixteenth notes, the last of which is tied over to the following downbeat (see, for example, the B strain of "Peace and Plenty Rag" or the B strain of "Sunburst Rag"), and to distinguish this motive from its more disjunct continuation.

In B1:2 and B1:10, the upper quarter-note stem could be played as written, since the f♯″ is consonant with the prevailing harmony (one could regard it as superfluous, however, since pedaling is likely to sustain the note in any case). Upper quarter-note stems are absent in B2:2 and B2:10. In addition, B2:10 in the original differs from B2:2 in the absence of a quarter note d″. This has been emended to follow not only B2:2 but also B1:2 and B1:10.

It is likely that the dynamic markings found in A1:4–8 (crescendo to *f* in m. 5, decrescendo in m. 8) apply to A2:4–8 as well.

The slur covering the ascending four-note motive in B1:1 (and its inversion in B1:8) should probably be understood to apply to all other instances of the same motive (B1:2, 3, 6, 9, 10, 11; B2:1, 2, 3, 6, 8, 9, 10, 11).

Pegasus

CRITICAL NOTES

A:5	LH, beat 2, second octave, both notes have ♯.
A:8	LH, beat 2, second octave, top note has ♯.
A:13	LH, beat 2, second octave, both notes have ♯.
B1:15	LH, beat 2, first eighth is quarter note.
C:7	LH, beat 2, second octave, top note has ♮.
B2:15	LH, beat 2, first eighth is quarter note.

COMMENTS

There are some curious inconsistencies in the use of broken left-hand octaves, which occur in measures 2, 4, 10, and 12 of the B strain. In B1 measures 2, 4, and 10 have three broken octaves (as indicated by grace notes tied to the bottom note of the octave); in B1:12 the last octave lacks the grace note. In B2 the situation is quite different: measure 2 has three broken octaves, while B2:4, 10, and 12 have two. It is likely that the grace notes have simply been haphazardly applied and that *all* of these measures should have three broken octaves. But lacking any corroborating evidence, these discrepancies have been retained.

The crescendo in A1:16b and B2:16a probably applies to the identical single-note run in B1:16a. The dynamic markings in B1 (crescendo in B1:4 and 12, decrescendo in B1:8) probably apply to B2 as well.

It is likely that each of the three descending left-hand octaves in B should carry accent marks, as in B1:11–12. Such accents are missing on the third octave in B1:2, B1:4, B1:10, and B2:4.

Don't Jazz Me—Rag

CRITICAL NOTES

A1:1	Thin-thin double barline at beginning, no repeat bar.
A1:6	RH, beat 2, second sixteenth, no ♮.

A1:10   RH, beat 1, third sixteenth, dyad c″–e″—emended after A2:10.

A1:12   LH, beat 1, second eighth, second note from bottom of chord, no ♯.

A1:13   LH, beat 2, second octave, bottom note, no ♯.

A1:15   RH, lower voice, beat 1, sixteenth chord, top note, no ♮; LH, beat 2, second eighth, middle note of chord, no ♯.

B1:1   No repeat bar.

B1:6   RH, beat 1, appears as follows—emended after B2:6:

B1:15   LH, beat 1, second eighth, chord is g–b–f′—emended after B2:15 and A2:15.

A2:8   LH, beat 1, second eighth, top note of chord, no ♮.

A2:9   LH, beat 2, second octave is G–g—emended after A1:9.

A2:12   RH, beat 2, note 3, no ♮.

C:2   RH, occupied by eighth-note chord, eighth rest, quarter rest; LH, beat 2, second eighth, an eighth rest appears above octave GG♯–G♯.

C:5   RH, beat 2, occupied by two eighth-note chords—emended after C:13.

C:8   LH, beat 1, second note from bottom of chord is a.

C:10   RH, occupied by eighth-note chord, eighth rest, quarter rest; LH, beat 2, second eighth, an eighth rest appears above octave GG♯–G♯.

C:12   RH, beat 1, fourth chord, second note from top is b♭′, beat 2, first sixteenth, chord is d′–f♯′–d″.

B2:14   RH, beat 2, second chord, second note from top, no ♭—emended after B1:14.

COMMENTS

There are minor discrepancies between the two versions of the A strain. In A1:4 the second left-hand octave on beat 2 is d♯–d♯′; in A2 it is c♯–c♯′. Both are within the bounds of possibility (although the C♯ octave is more dissonant). The left-hand chords of A1:8 have a d♮′ that is missing from the same chords in A2.

The numerous dynamic markings within B1 are de-

signed primarily to distinguish between the main melodic material and its "echo" in the upper register, to be played more softly. The performer would be well-advised to continue this practice in the B2 strain, although dynamic markings are lacking.

The right-hand slurs in B1:1, 9 likely apply to the corresponding measures in B2. In the C strain accent marks for the left-hand octaves are haphazardly applied. Since it seems likely that Scott wanted to bring out the stepwise motion in the bass across the barline wherever it occurred, the accent marks found in C:6–7, 10–11, and 13–14 should apply to the corresponding passages in C:14–15, 2–3, and 5–6, respectively.

Victory Rag

CRITICAL NOTES

Intro:1   LH, anacrusis, no sixteenth rest.

Intro:2   LH, beat 1, note 2, dyad a–c′.

A1:1   Thin-thin double barline at beginning, no repeat bar.

B1:1   Thin-thin double barline at beginning, no repeat bar.

B1:14   RH, beat 2, first chord, bottom note is b′—emended after B2:14.

A2:2   LH, beat 2, first octave is G–g—emended after A1:2.

A2:4   LH, beat 1, bottom note of chord has ♯.

C:1   Thin-thin double barline at beginning, no repeat bar; RH, beat 1, no half note—emended after C:3, 9, 11.

B2:1   No repeat bar.

B2:9   LH, beat 1, second eighth, chord is f–a–c♯′–e′, no ties to chord on beat 2—emended after B1:9—beat 2, first eighth, chord does not include g′—emended after B1:9.

B2:14   RH, last chord, no ties to downbeat of B2:15a.

B2:15b   RH, beat 1, no continuation ties from B2:14.

COMMENTS

The discrepancy in the notation of measures 11–12 between A1 and A2 has been retained, since the musical result is identical.

The left-hand octaves on the first beat of B1:6 and 8 do not appear in the corresponding measures of B2. This discrepancy is probably a conscious variation.

The dissonant cross relation in measure 14 of the B

strain, between f♯″ in the right hand and f♮′ in the left hand, appears to be intentional.

Strain A1 lacks a dynamic marking. A level of *mf*, as in A2, seems logical and appropriate.

In B1:1 and 3, the left-hand slurs extend to the following downbeat; in B2:1 and 3, they do not. The B1 slurs seem more appropriate. The slurs over the last three sixteenth notes in Int:4, C:2, 10, and 12 probably apply to the same motive in C:4, 6, 8, 14, and 16 (first ending).

Broadway Rag

CRITICAL NOTES

Intro:4	Single barline at end.
A1:1	No repeat bar.
A1:12	RH, upper voice, no eighth rest.
A1:15a, 15b	RH, beat 1, third chord, middle note, no tie to middle note of chord on beat 2.
A1:15b	LH, beat 1, lower note has continuation tie.
B1:1	No repeat bar.
B1:15a, 15b	RH, beat 1, third chord, middle note, no tie to middle note of chord on beat 2, beat 2, last chord, second note from bottom, no ♮.
A2:1	Single barline at beginning.
A2:12	RH, upper voice, no eighth rest.
A2:15	RH, beat 1, third chord, middle note, no tie to middle note of chord on beat 2, beat 2, last chord, second note from bottom, no ♮.
Int:1	RH and LH, beat 2, third octave, no ♮s.
Int:3	LH, beat 2, third octave, no ♮s.
C:1	RH, beat 1, no continuation ties.
B2:1	No repeat bar.
B2:3	RH, beat 1, third chord, middle notes of chord, no ties to middle notes of chord on beat 2.
B2:15a	LH, beat 1, top note of chord has upward flag, beat 2, note 2 has ♮.
B2:15a, 15b	RH, beat 1, third chord, middle note, no tie to middle note of chord on beat 2, beat 2, last chord, second note from bottom, no ♮.
B2:15b	LH, beat 1, top note of chord has upward stem.

COMMENTS

The dynamic marking for A2 is lacking. Either a continuation of the *f* of B or a return to the *mf* of A1 seems appropriate.

The slur over A1:11–12 probably applies to the corresponding measures in A2.

WALTZES

Valse Venice

CRITICAL NOTES

Intro:1–3	LH, no rests.
Intro:4	Single barline at end.
A1:32	LH, half rest.
B:15a	LH, occupied by quarter-note dyad (GG–F) and two quarter rests.
B:16a	LH, occupied by quarter rest and half rest.
B:16b	LH, no continuation slur and tie.
A2:1	Single barline at beginning.
C:1	LH, anacrusis, half rest.
C:21	RH, upper voice, bottom note is half note, lacks dot.
A3:23	LH, beat 2, chord lacks stem.
A3:28	LH, beat 3, no quarter rest.
A3:29	RH, appears as follows—emended after A1:29, A2:29:

A3:30	LH, beat 1, half note lacks dot.

COMMENTS

In the first three bars of the Intro, the lower staff is entirely blank. Rests have been added to clarify the role of the left hand.

In A:9, A1 and A2 have a half-note chord in the left hand on beat 2, while A3 has a quarter-note chord followed by a quarter rest. The latter reading seems more consistent with the accompaniment throughout the strain.

The chord in the right hand on beat 2 of C:3 differs slightly from the corresponding chord in C:11.

The notation for the left-hand part in A:5–6 and A:21 is idiosyncratic and somewhat misleading. The double stem on the half note on beat 1 would suggest a division into two voices, but the chord that falls on the second beat of the measure cannot belong to either of the two voices, since it overlaps the half note. Scott probably used the double stem simply as a way of encouraging the performer to bring out the bass voice, especially in the chromatic descent in measures 5–6. (The absence of a double stem in A2:6 is presumably an oversight.)

A different notation of the same rhythm appears in A3:5. The division into two voices suggested elsewhere is here made unambiguous. The half note with stem down belongs to the lower voice, while the chord on beat 2, carefully distinguished by surrounding quarter-note rests and by an upward stem, constitutes the upper voice. The discrepancies between these versions of the left-hand rhythm have been retained in this edition, since the musical result is virtually the same in either case.

The presence of a half-note G on beat 1 of A3:22—where the corresponding measures in A1 and A2 have a quarter note—is more problematic, since the change in note value produces a slightly different rhythm. But given the lack of evidence to support one reading over the other, this discrepancy has also been retained.

In two places (B:16a, C:1, anacrusis), a half rest was used. In accordance with the usual procedure for $\frac{3}{4}$ time, each half rest has been replaced by two quarter rests.

The dynamic level of *mf* at the beginning of A3 probably applies as well to A1 and A2, which lack a dynamic marking.

Articulation in "Valse Venice" is highly inconsistent. In some places the main motive of the A strain is grouped under one slur (as in the very beginning of the Intro). In others the four eighth notes are slurred as a unit, and occasionally the slur is omitted entirely. The longer slur makes the most sense musically and should be used as a guide for interpretation in A:1–3, 8–11, 16–19, and 24–29:

Shorter slurs over the three-note groupings in A:3–6, 11–14, and 19–22 are absent (and presumably inadvertently omitted) in A1:6, A1:22, A2:6, and A2:22. The bass slur found in A:15–16 is lacking in A3. Measures 30–31 in A3 lack the right-hand slurs found in A1:30–31 and A2:30–31, while the left-hand slurs do not, as before, involve the lower voice. Elsewhere in the A strain, accent marks are used consistently to highlight the melody on beat 1 of A:5–6, 13–14, and 21–22 but are absent in A2:13 and A3:21–22. Staccato marks are used consistently on beat 1 of A:25–27 but are absent in A2:25 and A3:26–27.

In the B strain the two right-hand quarter-note octaves in measures 4, 6, 8, 12a, and 16a are sometimes connected by slurs, sometimes not. These slurs are followed in subsequent measures by accents in the right hand on beat 1 of B:3, 5, 7, and 9 (but not B:1 or 11, where an accent mark would seem equally justified). Accent marks also appear in the left hand on beat 1 in B:3 and 5, but nowhere else; very likely, the bass notes should be accented in B:1, 7, 9, and 11 as well. In B:15b the slur (and tie) in the left hand has been extended to connect with beat 1 of the following measure. The presence of this slur strongly suggests that similar slurs in the right hand of B:15b were inadvertently omitted.

In the C strain the slurs covering the symmetric eight-bar phrases inexplicably fall short, ending, for example, in C:6, even though the phrase clearly does not end until the b♭′ of C:7–8.

Hearts Longing

CRITICAL NOTES

A1:2, 4	RH, lower voice, no quarter rests.
A1:6	RH, upper voice, note 4 has ♯, lower voice, beat 2, lower note has ♯, upper note, no ♯.
A1:8, 10, 12	RH, lower voice, no quarter rests.
A1:16, 18, 20	RH, lower voice, no quarter rests.
A1:24, 26	RH, lower voice, no quarter rests.
A1:28	RH, lower voice, no quarter rests, upper voice, note 3 has ♯; LH, beat 1, bottom note of chord, no ♯.
A1:32a	RH, lower voice, no quarter rests, repeat dots from A1:32b.
A1:32b	Marked "Fine."; RH, beat 1, g′ only, no tie; LH, beat 1, top note, no continuation slur.
B1:1	No repeat bar; RH, lower voice, beat 2, no quarter rest.
B1:2	RH, lower voice, beat 2, no quarter rest.
B1:4	RH, upper voice, beat 3, no quarter rest.
B1:5, 6	RH, lower voice, beat 2, no quarter rest.
B1:8, 12	RH, lower voice, no quarter rests.
B1:17–18	RH, lower voice, beat 2, no quarter rest.
B1:20	RH, upper voice, beat 3, no quarter rest.
B1:21–22	RH, lower voice, beat 2, no quarter rest.
B1:23	LH, beat 1, octave is F♯–f♯.
B1:24, 28	RH, lower voice, beat 3, no quarter rest.
B1:32b	Marked "D.S. 𝄋 to Fine."
C:1	RH, note 2 is e′—emended after C:5, 9.

C:14a	RH, beat 3, second eighth, bottom note has ♯.
B2:1	RH, lower voice, note 1 is g′.
B2:4, 6	RH, upper voice, beat 3, no quarter rest.
B2:18	RH, lower voice, beat 2, no quarter rest.
B2:20	RH, upper voice, beat 3, no quarter rest.
B2:21	RH, lower voice, beat 2, no quarter rest.
B2:22	RH, upper voice, beat 3, no quarter rest.
A2:2, 4	RH, lower voice, no quarter rests.
A2:5	RH, lower voice, beat 3, no quarter rest.
A2:6	RH, lower voice, beat 2, lower note, no ♮, beat 3, no quarter rest.
A2:8, 10	RH, lower voice, no quarter rests.
A2:12, 16	RH, lower voice, no quarter rests.
A2:17	RH, upper voice, no tie to m. 18.
A2:18, 20	RH, lower voice, no quarter rests.
A2:22	RH, lower voice, beat 3, no quarter rest.
A2:24, 26	RH, lower voice, no quarter rests.
A2:28	RH, lower voice, no quarter rests; LH, beat 1, bottom note of chord, no ♯.

COMMENTS

The original chord on beat 1 of A:28 in both of its appearances is extremely unlikely:

One solution would be to delete the accidental from a′, resulting in an A7 chord. But the solution adopted in this edition (adding a ♯ to a) creates a diminished seventh chord, which seems more in keeping with the style.

There are a number of minor irreconcilable discrepancies between the two appearances of the A strain. In the left hand the downbeat of the measure is variously a single note (A1:1–4, 17–21, 23, 25, 27, 30; A2:4, 20, 23) and an octave (A1:5–16, 22, 29; A2:1–3, 5–19, 21–22, 25, 27, 29). In A1:22 the bass octave on beat 1 is B–b, and the lower note of the chord on beat 2 is f♮; in A2:22 the bass octave is G–g, and the lower note of the chord is d.

In the A strain the composer has been careful to distinguish in the right-hand part between the melody (written with stems up) and the inner voice (stems down). Where the inner voice is silent, rests are present to preserve its independence. Exceptions to this are recorded in the critical notes above; in all cases rests have been added in the edition.

A similar situation pertains in the B strain, with the difference that the melody begins below the "inner voice" and is primarily written with stems down. Quarter rests have been added to beat 2 of B1:1, 2, 5, 6, 17, 18, 21, 22, and B2:18, 21.

There are a number of differences in left-hand and right-hand chord voicings in the two versions of the B strain. While B1 is in the tonic, B2 is in the subdominant; and the changes seem to be attributable to adjustments made for the difference in register.

Dynamic markings are lacking in all strains except B1, which is marked *mf*. This dynamic level seems appropriate (with expressive variation) for the entire waltz.

Slurring is highly inconsistent in the two appearances of the B strain. The slurs over the paired eighth notes on beat 3 in B1:1, 2, 8, 17, 18, 21, 22, and B2:1, 2, 4, 5, 6, 12, 17, 18, 22 imply similar slurs in B1:4, 5, 6, 12, 20, 24, and B2:8, 20, 21, 24. The slur that connects the two quarter notes of B1:16 with beat 1 of B1:17 seems the most plausible. It would apply to A1:32b–B1:1, C:16b–B2:1, and B2:16–17 and would supersede the two-note slur in B1:32a. The slur over the last three eighth notes of B2:29 implies a similar slur in B1:29.

The formal plan for "Hearts Longing" is obscured in the original by a confusing and clearly erroneous set of instructions. After playing the A1 and B1 strains twice, the performer is directed, by the indication "D.S. 𝄋 to Fine," to return to the beginning of the A1 strain and to play until the "Fine" in the second ending (A1:32b). But this ends the piece prematurely. There is still the entire C strain and recapitulation of the B and A strains to come. Scott must have intended for the performer to continue on to the C strain; and indeed, rising chromatic motion d′–d♯′ in A1:32b flows seamlessly to the e′ at the beginning of the interlude. The overall form is thus: Intro–A1–B1–A1–Int–C–B2–A2.

To make this form clear to the performer, we have eliminated the indication "Fine" in its two appearances: at the end of B1 (where it accompanied the "D.S." indication), and in the second ending of A1. To direct the performer to move from the last appearance of A1 to the interlude, we have added the indication "[2nd time: to Int]."

The Suffragette

CRITICAL NOTES

A1:1	Thin-thin double barline at beginning, no repeat bar.

A1:14	RH, last note, no ♮.
A1:16	LH, beat 2, bottom note of chord, no ♭.
B:1	No repeat bar.
B:16b	RH, beat 2, top note of chord, no ♭.
C:1	No repeat bar.
C:7	RH, note 2, no ♮—emended after C:23.
C:8	RH, beats 2 and 3, bottom note of chord (c′) lacks ledger line.
C:32b	LH, beat 1, no tie.
A3:14	RH, note 1, no ♮, last note, no ♮.
A3:15	RH, beat 3, top note has ♮.
A3:16	LH, beat 2, bottom note of chord, no ♭.

COMMENTS

In A1 and A3 a natural sign was omitted on the last note of measure 14 in the original. The e♮′ fits better within the prevailing sonority of G major and explains the presence of an otherwise superfluous flat on beat 1 of the following measure.

Accent marks in the right hand are used consistently in A1 but are absent in corresponding measures in A3 (A3:4, 8, 16, 20, and 24) and in A2:4. Left-hand accents are absent on beat 1 of A2:11 and 12. Slurs covering the right-hand figuration in A1:25–28 are missing in A3:25–28.

The slurs in the right hand of C bear little relationship to the actual phrasing of the melody. With the exception of C:13–16 and 28–32, the phrases should probably be grouped in four-bar units: C:1–4, 5–8, 9–12, and so forth. Similar phrasing for the left hand is begun in C:1–3 but is left incomplete (a remnant of a slur remains attached to the left hand in C:20). Accent marks to bring out the left-hand line in C:8–9 probably apply to C:24–25 as well.

Springtime of Love

CRITICAL NOTES

Intro:10, 12	RH, beat 3, bottom note has ♯.
A1:19	RH, upper voice, g″—emended after A2:19 and A3:19.
B:11	LH, lower voice, dotted quarter note.
A2:18	RH, upper voice, ambiguously notated as dotted half or dotted quarter note.
C:10	RH, lower voice, beat 2, ♮ from bottom note of chord.
A3:32	Thin-thin double barline at end.

COMMENTS

The eight-bar phrases of the A strain follow a consistent pattern of dynamic markings: *mp* for the first four eighth notes (the anacrusis) and *p* (presumably *subito piano*) for the first full measure. This pattern should probably be followed, even where the markings are incomplete. Markings for *p* are lacking in A1:17; A2:9 (although the decrescendo hairpin in A2:8 effectively substitutes for it), 17; and A3:9, 17. The marking for *mp* is lacking in A2:16.

The slur in A2:5–6 should probably extend to beat 1 of A2:7 (as in A1:5–7). A similar slur is lacking in A3:13–15. The slur in C:21–22 should probably extend to beat 1 of C:23 (as in C:5–7).

To judge from the variety of tempo markings in this waltz, considerable variance is expected throughout. The indication "Tempo I" appears in both A2 and A3, indicating either a ritardando in the measures immediately preceding or a change of tempo for the entire preceding strain. The marking "Brilliant" for the B strain may well be faster than "Daintily," while "Dolce" for the C strain may well be slower (the "a tempo" indication notwithstanding). There is a second "a tempo" marking within the C strain (C:17), suggesting a slackening of the pace for the chords in C:14–16.

SONGS

She's My Girl from Anaconda

CRITICAL NOTES

Verse:4	Single barline at end.
Verse:6	V, note 2 lacks dot.
Verse:10	V, *ossia* note 2 lacks dot.
Verse:12	V, note 5 is b♭′.
Verse:13	V, no quarter rest.
Verse:15	V, "planed."
Verse:20	V, "we'r."
Verse:21	RH, beat 2, second note from bottom of chord is a♭′.
Verse:22	V, note 2 is quarter note; RH, occupied by half-note chord only; LH, last octave is quarter note.
Chorus:1	LH, anacrusis, no sixteenth rest.
Chorus:4	V, no quarter rest.
Chorus:8	RH, beat 3, octave also includes e♭‴.
Chorus:12	V, notes 2–3 are flagged separately, no extender line after "And"; V and RH, no quarter rest.

Chorus:15   RH, upper voice, no quarter rests.
Chorus:16a   RH, third chord is dotted quarter note.
Chorus:16b   Marked "D.C."

Sweetheart Time

CRITICAL NOTES

Cr	"Jamas Scott."
Verse:6–7	V, half rest and quarter rest.
Verse:28	LH, beat 1, no ♭.
Verse:29	LH, beat 3, top two notes of chord have ♭.
Verse:32	LH, beat 1, no ♭.
Chorus:26	V, "untill"; LH, fermata from beat 2.
Chorus:27	V, "their."
Chorus:28	V, "its."

COMMENTS

The second quarter note in the vocal part of Verse:23 is probably intended to fit the extra syllable in the second verse. When singing the first verse, the performer should probably replace the g′ with a quarter rest, to make the passage conform with the characteristic rhythm of the verse.

In Verse:38, beat 2, there is a discrepancy between the piano part and the vocal line. It is likely that the b′ in the vocal line is a misprint and that d″ is intended.

The staccato marks in Chorus:3 should be applied to similar passages in Chorus:7, 19, and 23.

Take Me Out to Lakeside

CRITICAL NOTES

Verse:11	V, note 3 is g♯′—emended after Verse:27.
Chorus:16	RH, beat 1, no eighth rest.

COMMENTS

The two verses of this song are set to the same music, which may result in slight confusion in the three places where the number of syllables are not the same (Verse:8, 21, and 24). In each case the voice part has an extra note to accommodate the extra syllable. This notation has been retained from the original. The only confusion that might arise is in Verse:21, where the text "you" should probably be sung to a dotted half note c″ (as in Verse:13) rather than to the c″, b♭′ for the word "pleasures."

The Shimmie Shake

CRITICAL NOTES

Verse:2	LH, beat 2, middle note of chord has ♭.
Verse:10	V, "quite"; RH, first chord, second note from bottom, no ♭.
Verse:15	V, "its."
Verse:20	LH, beat 4, second octave, top note has ♭.
Chorus:4, 12–13	V, beat 4, *ossia* lacks dot.
Chorus:15	LH, occupied by eighth-note chord, eighth rest, quarter rest, half rest.
Chorus:16	RH, beat 2, grace note, no ♮; LH, half rest, eighth rest.
Chorus:26	V, note 2, no ♮.

COMMENTS

It is likely that the accent marks underneath the left-hand octaves in Verse:6–7 and elsewhere apply to similar passages: Verse:16–17, 18–19, 20–21; Chorus:16–17, 31a–1.

APPENDIX A

JAMES SCOTT PIANO ROLLOGRAPHY

Compiled and Edited by Michael Montgomery

A biography, filmography, or discography covers the life, films, or phonograph discs lived, acted in, or recorded by a specific personality or musician. In the same manner a piano rollography normally attempts to list all the player piano rolls played by a certain pianist (e.g., George Gershwin, Eubie Blake, Jelly Roll Morton). The rolls listed are the ones hand-played by the pianist in question.

Although James Scott made no piano rolls, we are nevertheless interested in the rolls issued of his compositions, whether hand-played (by anyone) or arranged, whether original ("vintage") or "recut." This James Scott rollography, the first comprehensive one to be compiled, is really a list of James S. Scott compositions appearing in the form of player piano rolls.

A piano rollography of this type is useful to collectors of piano rolls (and owners of player pianos) because it shows the different rolls of Scott rags that, with luck or diligence, may be obtained. Most people referring to this section of the edition will not be collectors, but they will be able to get a feel for how popular Scott's rags were with the music-buying public of the 1910–20 era.

One can see that there were a great many piano roll manufacturers (and there were more that do not appear in this list). The reason is simply that there were a great many piano dealers and a great many player piano roll customers. Ragtime was popular, and the "good" rags—those that were well syncopated and melodic (as Scott's were)—attracted a sizable audience. The most popular rags were first of all promoted by Stark, who mailed sheet music copies to piano roll firms, inviting them to produce rolls. After 1 July 1909 roll makers needed to pay royalties, so it made sense to promote as many issued rolls as possible.

Each roll company had arrangers who took music manuscripts or published numbers and transferred the notes to perforated rolls. These "arranged" rolls could be produced fairly quickly (if not always completely accurately) and fairly cheaply. Each company needed its own arranging identity, and so a comparison of any two arranged rolls shows subtle differences—not in the melodic line or harmony of the piece but in the number of notes that went down. Some roll arrangements were more orchestrated than others, some used doubling of octaves, some used tasteful obbligatos, but each roll had to be a little different. The roll companies watched each other carefully and could easily detect when another company "copied" someone's arrangement, so few rarely did.

253

By 1912–13 the major companies had perfected recording devices that captured the real-time playing of roll artists. This was the birth of the "hand-played" roll industry, and hand-played rolls gave the companies a greater marketing edge against competitors.

As popular as certain of Scott's rags were before 1920 (e.g., "Climax Rag," "Frog Legs Rag," "Grace and Beauty," "Hilarity Rag," and "Ragtime Oriole"), the roll collectors of the 1950s (and beyond) found it difficult to locate originals of even these hit numbers. It was inevitable that the few originals that surfaced would be duplicated to satisfy demand, and this is exactly what happened. "Recuts" are exact copies of originals made by special roll-reading and roll-duplicating machinery. An original roll is used as a master, and multiple duplicates—or recuts—are made as the original feeds slowly through a sensor-reader device.

Most roll recuts have always been cottage industry efforts. Although some recut rolls bear official-sounding company names, the recutters sell their wares to collectors as a sideline business. All recuts are limited editions. Many today are out-of-print, too, like the originals from which they were made. As can be seen, the volume of different James Scott rolls that has emanated from the various recutters/dealers indicates a steady interest in James Scott's music.

The following collectors and researchers gave substantial assistance for this rollography: Rob DeLand, Palatine, Illinois; Frank Himpsl, Freehold, New Jersey; Mike Schwimmer, Lake Bluff, Illinois; Ed Sprankle, Oakland, California; Trebor Tichenor, St. Louis, Missouri; and Dick Zimmerman, Grass Valley, California.

ROLL LABELS AND ABBREVIATIONS

Original Rolls

Original rolls are "vintage" piano rolls made between 1895 and 1930 as well as "contemporary" piano rolls produced between 1950 and the present that represent the first appearance or performance of a particular Scott composition.

A. Vintage roll labels and abbreviations (1895–1930)

Ae	Aeolian (Aeolian Company, New York)
Ang	Angelus Melodant Artistyle (Wilcox & White, Meriden, Conn.)
Art	Artempo (Bennett & White, Newark, N.J.)
Cap	Capitol (Capitol Music Roll Co., Chicago)
Col	Columbia (Columbia Music Roll Co., Chicago)
Con	Connorized (Connorized Music Rolls, New York)
Dom	Dominant (Connorized Music Rolls, New York)
88N	Eighty-Eight-Note (Aeolian Company, New York)
Electra	Electra (Standard Music Roll Co., Orange, N.J.)
FS	Full Scale (possibly American Piano Co., New York, using Electra masters)

Key	Keynote (Musicnote Roll Co., Dixon, Ill.)
Kib	Kibbey (Kibbey Manufacturing Co., Chicago)
Kim	Kimball (W. W. Kimball Co., Chicago)
Lyric	Lyric (Lyric Music Roll Co., Cincinnati)
M-A	Metro-Art (Aeolian Company, New York)
M-Dee	Mel-O-Dee (Aeolian Company, New York)
Mel	Melographic (Melographic Roll Co., Buffalo)
M-R	Master-Record (National Music Roll Co., St. Johnsville, N.Y.)
M-T	Metrostyle or Metrostyle Themodist (Aeolian Company, New York)
Mus	Musicnote (Musicnote Roll Co., Dixon, Ill.)
OH	Otto Higel (Otto Higel Co., Ltd., Toronto)
Pia	Pianolin (Rudolph Wurlitzer Co., North Tonawanda, N.Y.)
QRS	QRS (QRS Company, Chicago, New York, and Buffalo)
Roy	Royal (Royal Music Roll Company, Buffalo)
65N	Sixty-Five-Note (Aeolian Company, New York)
Sup	Supertone (U.S. Music Company, Chicago)
Un	Universal (Aeolian Company, New York)
Uni-Rec	Uni-Record Melody (Aeolian Company, New York)
USM	United States Music (U.S. Music Company, Chicago)
Wur	Wurlitzer (Rudolph Wurlitzer Co., North Tonawanda, N.Y.)

B. Contemporary roll labels and abbreviations (1950–91)

Bark	Barkerolle (rolls arranged and produced by Carl R. Barker)
CofR	Classics of Ragtime (rolls arranged and issued by Harold E. Boulware, Florissant, Mo.)
HPC	Hot Piano Classics (rolls arranged by John Farrell, issued by Mike Schwimmer)
PR	PianoRecord (Lyle Martin, South Pasadena, Calif.)
R-M	Ragmaster (John Farrell, Tingewick, England)

Recut Piano Rolls

Recuts are post-1950 copies (i.e., newly perforated duplicates) of original rolls (both vintage originals and contemporary originals).

AMR	Automatic Music Roll (Frank Adams, Seattle)
BJ	Ball Joint (Lee Valencia, San Francisco)
BT	Blues Tone (Rob DeLand, Palatine, Ill.)
CC	Collector's Classics (Don Rand, Los Angeles)
Echoes	Echoes (Ed Sprankle, Oakland, Calif.)
GA	Golden Age (Phil & Hazel Wenker, Riverside, Calif.)

Givens	Givens (Larry Givens, Wexford, Pa.)
HV	Hollywood Vintage Series (Steve Neilson, Los Angeles)
JC	Jazz Classics (Richard Riley, Greenwood, Calif.)
JM	Joel Markowitz (Joel Markowitz, Port Washington, N.Y.)
MS	Mike Schwimmer (Mike Schwimmer, Lake Bluff, Ill.)
Oleo	Oleoacres (George Fawkes, Olney, Ill.)
PR	PianoRecord (Lyle Martin, South Pasadena, Calif.)

ROLLOGRAPHY

Most rolls play eighty-eight notes (with perforations nine to the inch). When rolls shown are sixty-five note (with larger six-to-the-inch perforations), they are so designated. Dates following titles are copyright dates. Dates shown in the roll listings indicate the month and year of release to the buying public, when known. In a few cases dated catalogs help to determine that the rolls listed were issued at that time or earlier. Recut rolls are shown in parentheses after the originals from which they were made. "A" or "B" (etc.) after a recut number indicates first or second tune on a two-tune recut. MS recuts are numbered by auction number and item number, separated by a period. Thus, "200.4" means roll number 4 on auction number 200; no such number appears on the roll or box.

Broadway Rag (1922)
  CofR 0130 (JC 358, MS 158.1, BT 092B)

Calliope Rag
  R-M R39

Climax Rag (1914)
  Ae 104364 (65-note)
  Ang 91333
  Art 1857, played by Steve Williams (August 1915 or earlier)
  Cap A-1866, tune 9 (January 1925)
  88N 301037 (CC 135, CC 374B)
  M-T 104364 (65-note)
  M-T 301036
  OH X299 ("fox trot") (same as QRS 100395)
  Pia 797, tune 2
  QRS 100395, played by Max Kortlander (June 1916) (HV 1116, JM 30)
  Un 3010
  Un 100797 (65-note)
  Un 301037 (CC 135, GA 1186, BJ [no number])
  USM 66433 (April 1914)

Dixie Dimples (1918)
  R-M R7

Don't Jazz Me—Rag (1921)
  CofR 0159 (JC 6618)
  HPC 100 (MS 200.4)

Efficiency Rag (1917)
  M-T 303152 (CC 275)
  Un 303153 (March 1917) (PR 204, JC 124, BJ [no number], CC 275)
  USM 8397B (April 1917) (HV 1027, MS 190.5)

Evergreen Rag (1915)
  Bark 005 (PR 354, HV 1022A)
  CofR 0155
  Kib, number unknown (December 1915)
  Kib Rag Roll 691, tune 3 (February 1916)
  QRS 32269 (Givens [no number], CC 309A)
  USM 7278B (December 1915 or earlier) (HV 1022)

The Fascinator (1903)
  CofR 0081 (JC 366)
  PR 302, an original roll transcribed and arranged by Ralph K. Mullins

Frog Legs Rag (1906)
  CofR 0145 (JC 360)
  Con 582 (CC 208, HV 1019)
  Con 4301 (65-note; a copy is dated "12/7/11" at end)
  Electra 76202 (February 1914 or earlier)
  Kim B5132
  Kim F6154, tune 5 of a six-rag medley, including "Hilarity Rag" (q.v.)
  Mel 0804
  QRS X3570 (65-note) (August 1907 or earlier)
  QRS 9762 (October 1960)
  USM 1255 (65-note)
  USM 4709 (65-note) (JC 246, includes "Frog Legs Rag" and "Polar Bear Rag" by George P. Howard)
  USM 61253

Grace and Beauty (1909)
  Ang 90969
  Con 20460, played by W. Arlington (JC 400, CC 447A)
  88N 300119 (CC 213)
  Electra 80260 (December 1912 or earlier) (PR 211, JC HF-1)
  FS 80260 (same as Electra 80260?)
  Kim C6317 (HV 1018)
  Lyric 2504
  M-T 300118
  M-T 102604 (65-note)
  QRS 31388, tune 2 of a five-tune medley
  QRS 33206, medley roll of several tunes
  QRS Cel 137, played by Max Morath (roll leader reads "Scott Joplin's Grace & Beauty")

Sup 832394

USM 3294B (65-note) (December 1911 or earlier) (PR 328)

USM 63294 (December 1911 or earlier) (AMR 117)

USM 65399F, tune 6 of a seven-rag medley, including "Hilarity Rag" (q.v.) (December 1915 or earlier) (JC 1007, JM 42, CC 43, JC 235, PR [no number])

USM 5162 (and 65162), tune 5 of medley (December 1915 or earlier)

USM 5399 (65-note), medley roll

USM A roll, 1011-8 (JC 183B)

Great Scott Rag (1909)

CofR 0146 (JC 361)

QRS 31138 (HV 1114, CC 309B)

Hilarity Rag (1910)

Ang 91069

Con 3056 (September 1915)

Dom 10492

Electra 80343 (April 1913)

Kim B5248 (and C5248) (HV 1023, PR 320, AMR 124)

Kim F6154, tune 6 of a six-rag medley, including "Frog Legs Rag"

M-T 103174 (and Ae 103174) (both 65-note)

M-T 300278 (and Ae 300278)

QRS 31379, a five-rag medley

Roy 4304 (June 1913)

65N 100017 (65-note)

Sup 845342

Un 300279 (Oleo [no number])

USM 4542B (65-note) (December 1911 or earlier)

USM 64542B (December 1911 or earlier) (PR 356, CC 417B, MS 078.1)

USM 65399F, tune 5 of a seven-rag medley, including "Grace and Beauty" (q.v.) (JC 1007, JM 42, JC 235, PR 214, CC 43, CC 343E)

Honey Moon Rag (1916)

Art 9935, played by Steve Williams (October 1916) (HV 1028, JC 403, BT 062)

CofR 0098 (PR 106, HV 1028A)

M-A 203008, played by Felix Arndt

M-Dee 203009, played by Felix Arndt (reissued after 1920)

M-T 203008, played by Felix Arndt

Uni-Rec 203009, played by Felix Arndt (December 1916)

USM 8143 (and USM 68143)

Wur 20371, tune 4 (N.B. this "Honey Moon Rag" is a composition by Abe Oleman; it was recut [with "New Era Rag"] on PR [no number] and HV 1186)

Kansas City Rag (1907)

CofR 0132 (JC 304; label erroneously credits Joplin as composer)

Con 4334 (65-note)

Con 1560

QRS 30566 (June 1909 or earlier) (HV 1115, Givens [no number])

QRS X3796 (August 1911 or earlier)

Modesty Rag (1920)

CofR 0019 (JC 334)

New Era Rag (1919)

CofR 0152 (JC 6619)

Wur 20371, tune 6 in a rag medley (see "Honey Moon Rag"; this arrangement of "New Era Rag" contains many errors) (PR [no number], HV 1186)

On the Pike (1904)

CofR 0157 (JC 6620)

Ophelia Rag (1910)

CofR 0099 (PR 264, JC 386)

USM 64138B (December 1911 or earlier) (JC 5, CC 193, HV 1020, Givens [no number], PR 307)

Paramount Rag (1917)

CofR 0037 (JC 346, PR 127, BT 092A)

Mus 1074

Peace and Plenty Rag

CofR 0050 (JC 351)

Pegasus (1920)

CofR 0073 (HV 1026, PR 103, PR 307)

The Princess Rag (1911)

CofR 0133 (JC 359)

USM 64846B (December 1911 or earlier)

Prosperity Rag (1916)

CofR 0075 (JC 303)

USM 7905 (MS 143.3, CC 335B)

Quality (1911)

Con 20461, played by W. Arlington (May 1917) (JC 207, JC 400)

Kim C6778, a medley roll

QRS 32226 (October 1915) (CC 133, CC 374A, HV 1087A)

QRS 32346, a medley roll

USM 5270 (and USM 65270B) (HV 1087B)

Rag Sentimental (1918)

Mus 1075

PR 300, an original roll transcribed and arranged by Timothy E. Westman (JC 39, HV 1021)

USM 8737 (March 1918)

The Ragtime "Betty" (1909)

CofR 0129 (JC 335)

Electra 76018 (a copy is dated "6/7/10" at end) (Echoes 179, HV 1117)

M-R 22

Ragtime Oriole (1911)

Ang 91182

Art 1898, played by Steve Williams (August 1915 or earlier) (PR 341, BT 019)

Con 10311, played by W. Arlington (July 1916) (JC 401, PR 334)

88N 300645 (Oleo [no number])

Electra 80353 (June 1913)

FS 80353

Kim C6787

M-Dee 300643

M-T 100345 (65-note)

M-T 300642

QRS 32228 (October 1915)

QRS 100278, played by Max Kortlander (December 1915; label erroneously shows composer as "White")

Un 100345 (65-note)

Un 300643

USM 5311C (65-note)

USM 5311C (88-note and odd, since USM generally preceded its eighty-eight-note roll numbers with "6")

USM 65311C (June 1913 or earlier) (HV 1024, CC 168, JC 123, PR 193, CC 335A)

A Summer Breeze (1903)

CofR 0156

Sunburst Rag (1909)

CofR 0158

Kim B6794 (a copy is dated "Aug 1915" at end)

PR 251, an enhanced arrangement of the original USM roll (below) done by Lyle Martin

Sup 822361

USM 2261 (65-note)

USM 62261B (December 1911 or earlier) (CC 207, HV 1025, GA 1002, PR 213, CC 417A, MS 190.6)

USM A-1052, tune 10 (JC 245, MS 090.1B)

Troubadour Rag (1919)

CofR 0166

Col 0-398, tune 6 of a ten-tune roll

Key/Mus 1175 (HV 1118, PR 210)

SELECTED DISCOGRAPHY

78 RPM

Brooks, Eric. "Climax Rag." Poydras 17. N.d.

——. "Grace and Beauty." Poydras 16. N.d.

——. "Hilarity Rag." Poydras 69. N.d.

George Lewis's Stompers. "Climax Rag." Climax 101. May 1943.

Jelly Roll Morton's New Orleans Jazzmen. "Climax Rag." Montgomery Ward M-8480. New York, 28 September 1939 (Mx 041360-1).

——. "Climax Rag." His Master's Voice B-9219. New York, 28 September 1939 (Mx 041360-2).

Johnson, Dink. "Grace and Beauty." AM 515. March 1946.

Parker, John W. (Knocky). "Grace and Beauty." Paradox 8. April 1949.

Rose, Wally. "Frog Legs Rag." Good Time Jazz GTJ 25. June 1950.

Rose, Wally, with Yerba Buena Jazz Band rhythm section. "Climax Rag." West Coast 116. May 1946.

——. "Sunburst Rag." West Coast 103. June 1946.

Sid Phillips and His Band. "Frog Legs Rag." HMV BD-6198. April 1955.

Sutton, Ralph. "Climax Rag." Down Home 8. November 1949.

——. "Frog Legs Rag." Down Home 9. November 1949.

——. "Grace and Beauty." Down Home 10. November 1949.

Sutton, Ralph, with the Eddie Condon Orchestra. "Grace and Beauty." Decca 27408. October 1950.

Tony Parenti's Ragtime Band. "Grace and Beauty." Circle 1030. November 1947.

Van Eps, Fred. "Grace and Beauty." Pathé Actuelle 021088. Ca. 28 September 1923 (Mx 70341).

——. "Grace and Beauty." Edison 51324. New York, 6 February 1924 (Mx 9366).

——. "Ragtime Oriole." Pathé Actuelle 021088. New York, ca. 28 September 1923 (Mx 70342).

——. "Ragtime Oriole." Edison 51324. New York, 6 February 1924 (Mx 9365).

Unidentified piano roll performance. "Grace and Beauty." Circle Records 4022. N.d.

Unidentified piano roll performance. "Hilarity Rag." Circle Records. N.d. (Mx MXSL-4).

Unidentified piano roll performance. "Quality." Circle 5005. N.d.

Unidentified piano roll performance. "Quality." Circle Records. N.d. (Mx MXSL-7).

Unidentified piano roll performance. "Ragtime Oriole." Century 4022. N.d.

Unidentified piano roll performance. "Ragtime Oriole." Century 4022. N.d. (Mx 413).

Zenith Six, The. "Climax Rag." Tempo A-145. May 1956.

33⅓ RPM

Albright, William. *Sweet Sixteenths: A Ragtime Concert.* Musical Heritage Society MHS 4578. (Works by Joplin, Lamb, Scott, Blake, Albright, and others)

An' All That Jazz. Superscope Cassettes no. 9. ("Frog Legs Rag," "Grace and Beauty")

Anderson, T. J., cond. *Classic Rags & Ragtime Songs.* Columbia Special Products for Smithsonian Institution P12974. 1975. ("Grace and Beauty," "Quality," "Ragtime Oriole")

Arpin, John. *Concert in Ragtime.* Scroll Records LSCR-101. ("Efficiency Rag," "Great Scott Rag")

———. *The Other Side of Ragtime.* Scroll Records LSCR-103. ("Sunburst Rag," "Troubadour Rag")

Ashwander, Donald. *They All Played Ragtime.* Jazzology Records JCE-52. ("Calliope Rag")

Black Eagle Jazz Band. *Black Eagle Jazz Band.* Onward Records OHF 1001. ("Climax Rag")

Bolcom, William. *Heliotrope Bouquet: Piano Rags.* Nonesuch H-71257. 1971. ("Pegasus")

———. *Pastimes & Piano Rags: Artie Matthews, James Scott.* Nonesuch H-71299. 1974. ("Efficiency Rag," "Great Scott Rag," "Modesty Rag," "New Era Rag," "Troubadour Rag")

Burbank, Albert, and Big Eye Nelson. "Climax Rag." American Music Unissued Series, Dan Records VC-7026. Unissued take, 20 July 1949.

Charters, Ann. *Essay in Ragtime.* Folkways Records FG 3563. 1961. ("Rag Sentimental," "Victory Rag")

Coffman, Bill, and Kathy Craig. *Concert Time at Old Town Music Hall.* Old Town Music Hall Records OTMH 101. ("Great Scott Rag")

Contemporary Ragtime Guitar. Kicking Mule Records KM-107. ("Grace and Beauty")

Dave Brennan's New Orleans Jazzmen. *Inn Swinger.* VJM Records LC 12. ("Hilarity Rag")

Dickie, Neville. *Rags and Tatters.* Contour Records 2870 190. ("Frog Legs Rag")

Dickie, Neville, Quentin Williams, and Pete Davis. *Ragtime Piano.* Saydisc SDL-1188. ("Grace and Beauty" [Dickie], "Hilarity Rag" [Davis])

Dukes of Dixieland, The. *Dukes of Dixieland.* Audiofidelity AUF 5928. ("Grace and Beauty")

Dykstra, Brian. *American Beauty.* Century-Advent Records. ("Evergreen Rag")

———. *The Riches of Rags.* Orion Records ORS-83449. ("Efficiency Rag," "Pegasus")

Ferrell, Betty. *Ragtime Reflections.* Ferrell-1. ("Great Scott Rag," "Ophelia Rag")

George Lewis's New Orleans Band. "Climax Rag." American Music Unissued Series, Dan Records VC-7021. Unissued take, 15 May 1943.

Hasse, John. *ExtraOrdinary Ragtime.* Sunflower Records 501. 1980. ("Frog Legs Rag")

Jasen, David, comp. *Piano Ragtime of the Forties* [1941–49]. Herwin 403. Ca. 1975. ("Climax Rag")

———, ed. *Ragtime Piano Revival.* Folkways RBF-49. ("Frog Legs Rag")

Jelly Roll Morton's New Orleans Jazzmen. "Climax Rag." *Hot Pianos, 1926–1940.* Historical Records HLP 29. Unissued take, New York, 29 September 1939 (Mx 0413660-1B).

Jenks, Glenn. *The Ragtime Project.* Bonnie Banks Records BB-103. ("Ragtime Oriole")

———. *The Ragtime Project.* Volume 2. Bonnie Banks Records BB-104. ("Troubadour Rag")

Jensen, John. *Piano Rags by James Scott.* Genesis GS 1044. 1974. ("Broadway Rag," "Calliope Rag," "Climax Rag," "Evergreen Rag," "Frog Legs Rag," "Grace and Beauty," "Honey Moon Rag," "Modesty Rag," "Paramount Rag," "Pegasus," "Prosperity Rag," "Quality," "Ragtime Oriole," "Sunburst Rag," "Troubadour Rag," "Victory Rag")

Johnson, Bunk. *The Last Testament of a Great New Orleans Jazzman.* Columbia Cl 829. ("Climax Rag")

Jones, Jazzou. *Riverboat Ragtime.* High Water Records HW 101. 1983. ("Calliope Rag," "Grace and Beauty")

Ken Colyers Jazzmen. *Ragtime Revisited.* Joy Records Joys 194. ("Grace and Beauty," "Ragtime Oriole")

Laibman, David, and Eric Schoenberg. *The New Ragtime Guitar.* Transatlantic Records TRA 253. ("Ragtime Oriole")

Larson, LeRoy. *Banjo Ragtime and Other Classics.* Banjar Records BR-1781. ("Calliope Rag")

Lawson-Haggart Jazzband. *Ragtime Jamboree.* Decca Records DL8199. ("Grace and Beauty")

Lewis, George. *George Lewis' Ragtime Jazz Band.* Jazzology Records JCE-27. ("Climax Rag")

———. *George Lewis' Ragtime Jazz Band.* Disc Jockey DJL-100. ("Climax Rag")

———. *Live at the Hangover Club, 1953–1954.* Dawn Club DC-12008. ("Climax Rag")

London Ragtime Orchestra. *London Ragtime Orchestra.* Stomp Off Records SOS-1081. ("Ophelia Rag," "Quality")

Love, Charlie. *The Love-Jiles Ragtime Orchestra.* Riverside Records, RLP-379. ("Frog Legs Rag," "Hilarity Rag")

Mitchell, Bill. *Ragtime Recycled.* Ethelyn Records ER-1750. ("Grace and Beauty")

Morath, Max. *Max Morath and His Ragtime Stompers*. Vanguard Records VSD 79440. 1981. ("Kansas City Rag")

——. *Max Morath Plays the Best of Scott Joplin and Other Rag Classics.*
Vanguard Records VSD 39–40. 1972. ("Evergreen Rag," "Grace and Beauty," "Hilarity Rag")

——. *Max Morath Plays "The Entertainer."* Arpeggio Records ARP 1204S. ("Grace and Beauty")

——. *Oh, Play That Thing*. Epic LN-24106. ("Climax Rag")

——. *The World of Scott Joplin*. Volume 1. Vanguard Records SRV-310. ("Broadway Rag," "Frog Legs Rag," "Ragtime Oriole")

——. *The World of Scott Joplin*. Volume 2. Vanguard Records SRV-351. ("Evergreen Rag")

Nadeau, Roland L. *Grace and Beauty: Classic American Ragtime*. Sounds of Northeastern CSRV 2625. 1979.

New Black Eagle Jazz Band. *Brians' Songs*. Cassette LE 1003. ("Climax Rag"—two versions)

——. *The New Black Eagle Jazz Band*. Stomp Off Records SOS-1054. ("Climax Rag")

New England Conservatory Ragtime Ensemble. *The Road from Rags to Jazz*. Golden Crest Records CRS 31042. ("Frog Legs Rag," "Grace and Beauty," "Hilarity Rag," "Ophelia Rag")

New Orleans Ragtime Orchestra. *Grace and Beauty*. Delmark DS 214. ("Grace and Beauty," "Sunburst Rag")

——. *New Orleans Ragtime Orchestra*. Pearl Records PLP-7. ("Grace and Beauty," "Sunburst Rag")

Nichols, Red, and the Five Pennies. *Blues and Old Time Rags*. Capitol Records T 2065. ("Climax Rag")

Ophelia Ragtime Orchestra. *Ophelia Ragtime Orchestra*. Stomp Off Records SOS-1108. ("Calliope Rag")

Papa Bue's Viking Jazz Band. *Plays Spirituals, Marches, Ragtime, Cakewalks, Blues, and Standards*. Storyville Records SLP 121. ("Climax Rag")

Parker, John W. (Knocky). *From Cakewalk to Ragtime*. Jazzology JCE 81. ("Grace and Beauty")

——. *Late Ragtime Piano*. Folkways RF-34. ("Grace and Beauty")

——. *Old Rags*. Audiophile AP 49. ("Climax Rag," "Frog Legs Rag")

——. *The Complete Piano Works of James Scott*. Audiophile AP 76–77.

Pavageau, Alcide. *Slow Drag's Bunch*. Jazz Crusade JC-2005. ("Climax Rag")

Philharmonische Cellisten Koln. *Ragtimes*. Wergo, DDR, SM 1016.

Phillips, Sid, and his band. *Sid Phillips*. Her Majesty's Voice BD 6198. April 1955.

Phoenix Symphony Ragtime Ensemble. World Jazz Records WJLP-S12. ("Grace and Beauty," "Frog Legs Rag," "Quality")

Pianola Ragtime. Saydisc Records SDL-132. ("Ragtime Oriole")

Piano Ragtime of the Forties—Pork and Beans. Herwin Records 403. ("Climax Rag"—Ralph Sutton)

Piano Rolls Ragtime. Sound Records Sounds-1201. ("Grace and Beauty")

Queen City Jazz Band. *Queen City Jazz Band*. Toad Records TR-2. ("Grace and Beauty")

Ragtime Piano Rolls. Jazz Piano JP 5001. ("Evergreen Rag," "Frog Legs Rag")

Rainier Jazz Band. *Live at Mom's*. Triangle Jazz Records Ltd. T-104. ("Climax Rag")

Rose, Wally. *Ragtime Classics by Wally Rose*. Good Time Jazz M12034. ("Frog Legs Rag")

——. *Rose on Piano*. Blackbird Records C12007. ("Peace and Plenty Rag")

Rummel, Jack. *Back to Ragtime*. Stomp Off Records SOS-1118. ("The Ragtime 'Betty'")

Scott Joplin 1916: Classic Solos Played by the King of Ragtime Writers and Others from Rare Piano Rolls. Biograph Records BLP-1006Q. ("Grace and Beauty," "Quality," "Ragtime Oriole")

Shields, Roger. *The Age of Ragtime*. Turnabout Records TV-S 34579. ("Ragtime Oriole")

Sokolow, Fred. *Ragtime Banjo Bluegrass Style*. Kicking Mule Records KM 212. 1980. ("Great Scott Rag")

Sutton, Ralph. *Backroom Piano*. Verve Records MGV-1004. ("Frog Legs Rag," "Grace and Beauty")

Sutton, Ralph, with Eddie Condon and His Orchestra. *Jazz Band Ball*. Decca Records DL 5196. 1951. ("Grace and Beauty")

Swift, Duncan. *Piano Ragtime*. Black Lion Records BL301. ("Climax Rag")

Taylor, Keith. *Ragtime Piano*. Sami Records TB-1001. 1981. ("Prosperity Rag")

Thompson, Butch. *Butch Thompson*. Minnesota Public Radio MPR 34817. 1979. ("Ragtime Oriole")

Tichenor, Trebor, and Michael Montgomery. *James Scott: Classic Ragtime from Rare Piano Rolls*. Biograph BLP-1016Q. 1975. ("Climax Rag," "Efficiency Rag," "Evergreen Rag," "Frog Legs Rag," "Grace and Beauty," "Great Scott Rag," "Hilarity Rag," "Honey Moon Rag," "Kansas City Rag," "Ophelia Rag," "Quality," "Rag Sentimental," "Ragtime Oriole," "Sunburst Rag")

Tony Parenti's Ragtimers. *Ragtime*. Jazzology Records J-15. ("Grace and Beauty")

Turk Murphy Jazz Band. *The Many Faces of Ragtime*. Atlantic S1613. 1972. ("Climax Rag," "Grace and Beauty")

Van Eps, Fred, and Vess L. Ossman. *Kings of Ragtime Banjo*. Yazoo Records 1044. ("Ragtime Oriole")

Waldo, Terry. *The Gutbucket Syncopators*. Stomp Off Records SOS-1032. ("Grace and Beauty")

Watts, Hugh. *Hugh Watts' Jeune Amis Jazz Band*. Polydor 623.222. ("Climax Rag")

Weatherburn, Ron, and Sandy Sanders. *Ragtime Piano*. Rediffusion Records 0100170. ("Grace and Beauty")

Yarra Yarra Jazz Band. *On Tour.* G.H.B. Records GHB-78. ("Climax Rag")

Zimmerman, Richard. *The Collector's History of Ragtime.* Murray Hill M-60556/5. ("Grace and Beauty")

Zukofsky, Paul, and Roger Dennis. *Classic Rags.* Vanguard Records SRV-350SD. ("Calliope Rag")

APPENDIX C

FOLIOS

Although the present edition is the first complete collection of Scott's works, many of his rags have appeared in folio:

The Best of Ragtime Favorites and How to Play Them. New York: Charles Hansen, n.d. ("Climax Rag," "Evergreen Rag," "Frog Legs Rag," "Grace and Beauty," "Hilarity Rag," "Honey Moon Rag," "Prosperity Rag," "Quality," "Ragtime Oriole," "Victory Rag")

Blesh, Rudi, comp. *Classic Piano Rags: Complete Original Music for 81 Rags.* New York: Dover, 1973. ("Broadway Rag," "Don't Jazz Me—Rag," "Efficiency Rag," "Evergreen Rag," "Frog Legs Rag," "Great Scott Rag," "Hilarity Rag," "Kansas City Rag," "Modesty Rag," "New Era Rag," "Paramount Rag," "Peace and Plenty Rag," "Pegasus," "Rag Sentimental," "The Ragtime 'Betty'," "Ragtime Oriole," "Sunburst Rag," "Troubadour Rag," "Victory Rag")

Golden Encyclopedia of Ragtime, 1900–1974. New York: Charles Hansen, 1974. ("Climax Rag," "Evergreen Rag," "Frog Legs Rag," "Grace and Beauty," "Hilarity Rag," "Honey Moon Rag," "Prosperity Rag," "Quality," "Ragtime Oriole," "Victory Rag")

N.B. "Hearts Longing," "The Shimmie Shake," "Springtime of Love," "The Suffragette," "Sweetheart Time," "Take Me Out to Lakeside," and "Valse Venice" have never been reprinted.

Hoefer, George, ed. *The Dixieland New Orleans Book #3: Blues, Stomps and Ragtime,* London: Herman Darewski Music Publishing Co., 1958. ("Climax Rag," "Grace and Beauty," "Hilarity Rag")

Jasen, Dave, ed. *Ragtime: 100 Authentic Rags.* New York: The Big 3 Music Corp., 1979. ("Ophelia Rag")

Morath, Max, ed. *One Hundred Ragtime Classics.* Denver: Donn Printing, 1963. ("Broadway Rag," "Don't Jazz Me—Rag," "Efficiency Rag," "Evergreen Rag," "The Fascinator," "Great Scott Rag," "Hilarity Rag," "Kansas City Rag," "Modesty Rag," "New Era Rag," "Ophelia Rag," "Paramount Rag," "Peace and Plenty Rag," "Pegasus," "Rag Sentimental," "The Ragtime 'Betty'," "Ragtime Oriole," "Sunburst Rag," "Troubadour Rag")

The Ragtime Folio: The Morris, Mayfair, Melrose Series of Famous Blues, Stomps, and Ragtime. New York: Melrose Music Corp., n.d. ("Climax Rag," "Frog Legs Rag," "Grace and Beauty," "Hilarity Rag")

Shealy, Alexander, ed. *World's Favorite Music and Songs; Ragtime.* Carlstadt, N.J.: Ashley Publications, 1973. ("Frog Legs Rag")

34 Ragtime Jazz Classics for Piano. New York: Melrose Music, 1964. ("Climax Rag," "Evergreen Rag," "Frog Legs Rag," "Grace and Beauty," "Hilarity Rag," "Honey Moon Rag," "Prosperity Rag," "Quality Rag," "Ragtime Oriole," "Victory Rag")

Tichenor, Trebor J., comp. *Ragtime Rarities: Complete Original Music for*

63 Piano Rags. New York: Dover, 1975. ("The Fascinator," "On the Pike," "A Summer Breeze")

———, ed. *Ragtime Rediscoveries: 64 Works from the Golden Age of Rag.* New York: Dover, 1979. ("Dixie Dimples," "Ophelia Rag," "The Princess Rag")

Zimmerman, Richard, comp. *A Tribute to Scott Joplin and the Giants of Ragtime.* New York: Sattinger-International Music, Charles Hansen, 1975. ("Dixie Dimples," "The Fascinator," "On the Pike")

ORCHESTRATIONS

"Calliope Rag." Arranged by LeRoy Larson. LeRoy Larson, 1980.

"The Fascinator." Arranged by E. W. Berry. Kansas City, Mo.: E. W. Berry, 1912.

"Frog Legs Rag." Arranged by Scott Joplin. St. Louis: Stark Music Co., ca. 1912.

"Grace and Beauty." Arranged by E. J. Stark. St. Louis: Stark Music Co., ca. 1912.

———. Arranged by Elmer Schoebel. Chicago: Melrose Brothers Music, 1926.

"Hilarity Rag." Arranged by Rocco Venuto. St. Louis: Stark Music Co., ca. 1912.

"Kansas City Rag." Arranged by Max Morath. New York: E. B. Marks Music Corp., 1981.

———. Arranged by W. and Lynn Butcher. Lynn Butcher, 1952.

"Ophelia Rag." Arranged by Rocco Venuto. St. Louis: Stark Music Co., ca. 1912.

INDEX